Good Manners for Success

Ibn Hibban

Published by Muddassir Khan, 2024.

Table of Contents

Good Manners

for Success

Ibn Hibban

Introduction

All praise belongs to Allah, the One who is unique in His divine power, the Mighty in the greatness of His Lordship, the Guardian of all creatures and their appointed times, the Knower of their changes and their conditions, the Provider of perpetual blessings, The Giver of abundant bounty, The One who gave life to creatures when He willed, without help or advice, who created humanity when He wished, without an equal or a peer.

His Will is exercised on them by His Power, His wish for them is implemented by His Power.

He inspired them to do good without limits and instilled in them good manners.

They therefore act according to their abilities, evolving through the branches of good morals.

They rejoice in what has been decreed and preordained, "each group rejoicing in its belief."

I testify that there is no god worthy of worship except Allah, Creator of the heavens and the earth and their splendors.

His Wisdom knows no bounds and no one can oppose His Command: He is not questioned about what He does, but it is they who will have to account [for their actions].

I testify that Muhammad is His chosen servant and His pleasing Messenger.

He was sent with an extended light, an empowering command passed on by all messengers, and lessons learned from their ways.

He resisted oppression, complemented the faith, manifested it above all other religions, and suppressed idol worshipers.

May Allah bless him and his family and grant them peace as long as the stars revolve in the sky.

Indeed, Allah is glorified in His kingdom.

As for what comes next, it is clear and obvious to the reasonable person that times are changing.

They are constantly fluctuating.

The udder dries out after being full.

The branches wither after flowering.

Strength disappears after being virile.

The taste becomes bitter after being sweet!

People have emerged claiming to master intelligence and wisdom using the opposite of what they imply, such as following the desires of their hearts.

They have abandoned the demands of intelligence for the anguish of their chests.

They believed that the foundations of reason included hypocrisy, sycophancy and their branches which can be seen in their representatives through their fine clothes and eloquent speech.

They claimed that the one who masters these elements is the one gifted with intelligence and worth following, while the one who possesses none of these traits is an idiot who should be avoided.

So, when I noticed that the scum of the earth dazzled, misled by their actions and that the loudmouths followed their example, I decided to write this modest work.

It contains elegant meaning that the intelligent and wise need today.

It is intended to be a guide to distinguish those gifted with discernment when they are present and from whom those gifted with understanding draw when they are absent.

Through it, the learned and attentive will be able to surpass their contemporaries and their peers.

This work will be, in private, an honest confidant for the wise man and a close protector in public.

Through it, he will be favored by his supporters and will surpass his opponents.

I clarify, in this book, what will beautify, in the eyes of the sane man, the practice of praiseworthy qualities and uglify the practice of condemnable faults while seeking to prevent the persistence in the accumulation of these faults, of lighten the weight of the wearer and illuminate the listener's ear.

Because of the many stories and poems that will be mentioned in this book, anyone who strives to study each chapter in depth will wish that they had no ending.

As for the one who refuses to achieve completeness and success, he will certainly have accepted weakness.

Allah is the Giver of success and the Guide to integrity.

I ask Him for rectification of the soul and forgiveness from punishment due to sins.

He is certainly the most Generous, Noble and Merciful.

Chapter 1: Intelligence

———

According to Sahl ibn Sa'd (Allah be pleased with him), the Prophet (peace and blessings of Allah be upon him) said:

"Surely, Allah loves the person of good behavior and dislikes the person of bad behavior."

Loving the person with good behavior and hating the person with bad behavior is the essence of wisdom.

Intelligence is an immense treasure: it makes exile pleasant and neutralizes poverty.

No wealth is better than it and an individual's religion cannot be complete without intelligence.

Intelligence is of two types: natural and acquired.

Natural intelligence is like the earth.

The acquired intelligence is like seeds and water.

It is impossible for natural intelligence to achieve an action without exposing it to acquired intelligence.

This, in order to wake it from its sleep and free it from its place, just as the seed and the water extract what is deeply rooted in the earth in order to make it bloom abundantly.

Thus, the natural intelligence deeply rooted in man is like the roots of the tree under the earth and the acquired intelligence is displayed like the fruits hanging from the branches of the tree.

Muhammad ibn Ishaq ibn Habib al-Wasiti recited this poem to me:

I realized that intelligence has two identities:

Learned and natural.

And acquired intelligence is of no use

Without the company of natural intelligence

Just like the sun is of no benefit

When for looks, its rays are prohibited from sight.

Intelligence and desire are two adversaries.

The individual must therefore support his reason and hinder his desires.

Thus, if two situations are ambiguous, he must abstain from what is closest to his desires.

By doing so, one's intentions will be purified, then through intelligence and reason, consciences will be rectified.

'Abd Al-'Aziz ibn Sulayman al-Abrash recited the following verses to me:

If a man perfects his intelligence, his affairs are perfected,

His benefits are perfected and His appearance is perfected.

So without intelligence, his shortcomings are displayed,

Even if he has the fortune of a rich man.

The sagacious man does not start a conversation unless he is asked a question.

He doesn't debate much, unless it's allowed.

He is not quick to give an answer unless there is certainty.

The wise man does not belittle anyone, because he who belittles the leader ruins his life, he who belittles the pious destroys his faith, he who belittles his brother damages their reputation and he who belittles the common people withdraws their protection.

Al-Muntasr ibn Bilal ibn al-Muntasr al-Ansari recited these verses to me:

Don't you see that intelligence beautifies its possessor

And that we perfect it through long experience?

And certainly, the past reprimands its owner,

Who improves every day through his knowledge.

The wise man grasps what he has never seen by comparing it to what he has seen.

He assigns what he has not heard to what he has heard.

He puts his mistakes and his successes side by side.

He applies his past to what remains of his life.

He connects what he never got to what he received.

He does not rely on money, even in need, because goods run out and disappear, while intelligence increases in value and does not disappear.

If intelligence were a tree, it would be the best kind, just as if patience were a fruit, it would be the best kind.

What increases intelligence brings closer to all the forms it can take and diverts everything that opposes it.

Wise people mix with people for one of two reasons:

· - to talk about a situation to which they need to draw attention,

- to inform the ignorant of something important that they need to know.

The sensible man seeks to benefit from all forms of intelligence and learns from what opposes it in every situation.

The intelligent person should not flatter the other, unless the latter is able to bear the flattery.

He should not give his attention to anyone unless this attention is appreciated.

If intelligence had parents, it would be patience and prudence.

Allah created us to be those who possess within us the magnificent presence of intelligence.

Thus, he who perfects this benefit has the qualities which will lead him to his Lord.

Indeed, he obeys Allah and accomplishes what He wants.

Chapter 2: Piety

According to Usamah ibn Sharik (Allah be pleased with him), the Prophet (peace and blessings of Allah be upon him) said: If Allah hates that you do something, then do not do it (even) when you are alone.

The sagacious man and the prudent man must know that reason is made up of branches composed of orders and prohibitions.

He must know them and perform them at their prescribed times, as a demonstration to the common people and the miscreants.

The first of the branches of reason is piety (Taqwa – consciousness of Allah), self-rectification, because whoever purifies his interior, Allah will purify his exterior, and whoever corrupts his interior, Allah will ruin his exterior.

Certainly, the one who said the following spoke the truth:

If you are isolated at some point during the day, don't say: "I am alone", but say: "A Vigilant Guardian sees me."

And do not think that Allah is heedless

Or that He doesn't see what we want to hide from Him.

Can't you see the days pass quickly

And tomorrow is near for those who are worried (who are heedful).

The wise person must give importance to improving his interior.

He must protect his heart when he is near and when he is far away, when he is active and when he is still, because his life is filled with difficulties and his joys are ruined when the heart is sick.

If there was no other reason than Allah exposing what is inside a person, whether good or bad, that would be enough for the intelligent to rectify and correct his inner self.

Muhammad ibn 'Abdillah ibn Zinji al-Baghdadi recited these verses to me:

If you display the good

So make what you hide even better

For he who conceals good is characterized by it

And he who conceals evil is characterized by it.

The wise man must rectify his person and keep away from sins using his piety and good works.

So, if his body does not act piously, he must reign over it and control it through his heart.

Indeed, the actions of the limbs are purified by the purification of the heart.

Mansur ibn Muhammad al-Kurayzi recited the following verses to me:

Without his heart and his tongue man is nothing else

In his communication and behavior.

And if a man's clothes are not clean,

It may be that even using water you are powerless (not able to purify it).

And you won't be touched (harmed) by everything that scares you

And you won't get everything you wanted.

The person gifted with reason must not forget to protect his heart from what hardens it, because if you rectify the king, you rectify the army, and if you corrupt the king, you corrupt the army.

Thus, faced with two situations, he must abstain from the one closest to his desires and pursue the one furthest from destruction.

Whoever recited the following poem was right:

If your heart is in conflict between two affairs,

So, choose the most decent and clear one.

If you're worried about a bad deal, be hesitant

If you're worried about a good deal, just do it.

Hearts are purified of their impurities when the individual is concerned only with Allah and everything becomes insignificant compared to the goal of satisfying Him through obedience, whether in solitude or in the company of others.

This is the best sustenance in this life and the next for those who are attentive (heedful).

Muhammad ibn Ishaq ibn Habib al-Wasiti recited this poem to me:

Fearing Allah is obligatory on you in all situations.

You will see the (good) consequences (of fearing Him alone) on the Day of Judgment.

Certainly, fearing Allah is the best conclusion,

And constitutes for the traveler the greatest provision.

Chapter 3: Knowledge

Zirr ibn Hubaysh is reported to have said: I went to Safwan ibn 'Asal al-Muradi who said to me: "What brought you here? ".

I replied: "I am in search of knowledge."

He said: "I heard the Messenger of Allah say: No one leaves his house for the purpose of seeking knowledge without the angels lowering their wings in approval of his act."

Once the wise man has rectified his person, he must couple this with the search for knowledge and perseverance on this path.

Indeed, there is no better way to clarify the affairs of this lower world for a person than the purity of knowledge.

A sensible man is not careless about something that causes angels to spread their wings over him in approval of what he has accomplished.

However, he should not hope that his efforts will bring him closer to kings or allow him to acquire material things.

There is nothing worse than a scholar who stoops to the level of the followers of this lower world (the worldly life).

Al-Fudayl ibn 'Iyad said: There is nothing worse than the scholar to whom the people of his region go and ask, "Where is the shaykh?", then they are told: "He is with the governor", or "He is with the judge."

So what does the judge have to do with the scholar? So what does the governor have to do with the scholar? The scholar must be in his mosque reading the Quran."

Muhammad ibn Muhammad ibn 'Abdillah ibn Zinji recited these verses (of poetry) to me:

In knowledge and Islam, the individual finds protection

And to abstain from an obedient heart is bondage.

Are apparent to the young, the flashes of guidance

And knowledge of good qualities is gained through experience.

The person gifted with reason does not sell his share of the beyond (hereafter) for knowledge in exchange for what he could obtain from the vanities of this world.

Indeed, the goal of the search for knowledge is not the acquisition of knowledge in itself.

The goal in anything is the benefit you get from it, not the thing itself.

However, knowledge and the benefit of knowledge are two distinct elements.

Therefore, he who omits his benefit will never be beneficial to himself.

He will be like the one who eats without ever being satisfied.

Knowledge therefore constitutes the beginning and the end for him.

Sufyan Al-Thawri said: "Knowledge begins with silence, then comes listening, then memorization, then putting it into practice and finally transmitting it."

Al-Abrash recited these verses to me:

Learn! Because the individual is not born wise

And the holder of knowledge is not like the ignorant.

The elder of the tribe has no knowledge near him

If the assembly, towards the young person, is all ears.

The wise man is only concerned with the search for knowledge when he intends to put it into practice.

Indeed, he who strives to acquire knowledge with a view to something other than what we have described will become more and more vain and arrogant.

His complacency will gradually increase and he will be careless towards his works.

Furthermore, his case will worsen due to his influence on those who follow him.

His example is like the Word of Allah: Let them therefore bear on the Day of Resurrection all the burdens of their own works and part of the burdens of those whom they unknowingly lead astray; how bad is [the burden] they carry!

Ahmad ibn Muhammad al-San'ani and Muhammad ibn 'Abdillah recited these verses of poetry to me:

Be careful ! They seek knowledge in every city

Young people, who when they find it, accumulate it

And its texts as well as its foundations are authenticated to them,

Then they become scholars who are careless and turn away,

They prefer life here below, and therefore drink in it.

O scholars of evil, where have your senses gone?

And where is the hadith chosen and supported?

The wise man must seek only the best of knowledge, because the increase in knowledge influences the sagacious individual through his memories.

Knowledge is an adornment in times of ease and a refuge in times of difficulty.

He who studies improves, just as he who has ambition becomes a leader.

Excessive knowledge of all that is bad is destructive, just as excess of good manners in order to please other than Allah is a great sin.

The person gifted with reason makes no effort in his field of activity without it being advantageous for him both for this life and for the next.

If, however, he receives a benefit, he is not stingy in the way he uses it.

I have never seen someone miserly with their knowledge without it being of any benefit to them, just as underground water tables are useless without extracting them from the ground, or red gold before it is extracted from its mine, or the precious pearl before it is extracted from its ocean.

Likewise, knowledge is of no use as long as it is hidden and not propagated or used.

Abu Al-Darda (Allah be pleased with him) said: "People are either teachers or students and there is no good in anything other than that."

Al-Kurayzi recited the following verses:

Take advantage of knowledge and don't be stingy with it. Use your knowledge wisely.

Use your knowledge as best you can

And be someone who acts with knowledge and who benefits people.

Whoever benefits them, Allah will reward him,

And Allah will set him free from those who do not benefit.

He who makes efforts for this is not weak.

Weak is only he who does not make efforts.

Chapter 4: The Silence

Narrated Abu Hurayrah (Allah be pleased with him), the Messenger of Allah (peace and blessings of Allah be upon him) said: Whoever believes in Allah and the Last Day, let him speak good or remain silent.

If the wise person puts into practice the last two tools I mentioned (piety and knowledge), then his efforts should turn to monitoring his tongue until it is rectified.

Indeed, language is a source of destruction for an individual.

Silence earns the person love and dignity.

He who holds his tongue brings peace to himself, because regretting having kept silence is better than regretting having spoken.

Silence is the sleep of intelligence and speech is its awakening.

Abu Al-Darda (Allah be pleased with him) said: "There is no good in life except one of two men: the silent and attentive man or the man who expresses himself with knowledge."

The sagacious man should not try to speak over others or interrupt them, for while speech spoken at the right time may be appreciated and important, silence at the right time is of a higher degree.

The individual is either a model of conduct or lost and carefree, depending on their language.

Allah, the Venerable and Almighty, has elevated the tongue above other parts of the body, for there is nothing that brings more rewards when used in obedience and nothing worse than it, in matters of sin, when it is used in disobedience.

Muhammad ibn 'Abdillah ibn Zinji al-Baghdadi recited the following verses of poetry to me:

If blame can be brought to you by what you say

Then silence is better, if in these words there is no profit.

Do not let any words appear from your tongue without taming it

By a reflection which preceded it (think before you speak).

The tongue has ten qualities that the wise man must know.

He must use each of them at the right time.

It is a tool of expression, a witness who informs about hidden thoughts, a speaker who answers a question, a judge who renders a decision, a mediator through whom you know the needs, an interpreter through whom you can understand things , a landscaper who removes hatred and hostility like weeds, a charmer who attracts love, a consoler which enlightens hearts, a comfort which repels sadness.

Al-Baghdadi Muhammad ibn 'Abdillah ibn Zinji recited the following verses:

Your silence against error is a shield

Excessive talking leads to worry.

Do not say a word and then say: "If only I had never said what I said."

The tongue of the wise man is behind his heart, so if he wants to express himself, he must first rely on in (his heart).

If it approves, then he speaks, otherwise he remains silent.

The heart of the ignorant is at the tip of his tongue, he says everything that comes to mind.

He who does not preserve his language does not understand his religion.

If the tongue is upright, it will show in its actions, just as if it is corrupt.

Al-Kurayzi recited the following verses:

Hide stuttering as much as you can with silence.

Indeed, it (silence) is a comfort to the person blessed with patience.

When you are uncertain, make it (silence) an answer.

Maybe his answer will be in your silence.

The intelligent protects himself from trouble at all times.

Now, one of the greatest corrupting disorders of the rectitude of the soul and one of the greatest causes of the disappearance of piety in the heart is excess of words.

The only way for a person to cultivate tranquility is to let go of the things that lead them to speak.

Chapter 5: Truthfulness

According to 'Abdullah ibn Mas'ud (Allah be pleased with him), the Prophet (peace and blessings of Allah be upon him) said:

"You must be truthful.

Truth leads to works of good and works of good leads to Heaven.

A man never stops speaking the truth until he is known to Allah as truthful.

Lying leads to immorality and immorality leads to Hell.

A man continues to lie until he is considered a liar by Allah."

Certainly, Allah the Noble, the Almighty, has favored the tongue over the rest of the parts of the body.

So, He elevated its status and made its superiority apparent by allowing it to speak of His Oneness.

Thus, the intelligent must not use in lies the tool created by Allah to express His Oneness.

Rather, he must continually accustom his tongue to speak the truth and accomplish whatever will benefit him in both abodes (this life and the hereafter).

Indeed, language dictates inclinations: if it is truthful, then it leads to truthfulness, if it lies, it leads to lies.

The poet who made the following remarks was certainly right:

Restrict your tongue to good words, the good you will have gained.

Language is conditioned by what it is used to.

It is a representative who asks for a judgment on what you prescribe to it

So, make a choice for yourself and see how you fare.

It is easy to beautify different parts of the body, but not the tongue.

Language can only be beautified by educating it and truthfulness saves while lies destroy.

Those who master their languages can become leaders among their own.

Someone who lies excessively leaves no room for honesty.

An individual only lies if he gives no importance to his own person.

Muhammad ibn Ka'b al-Qurzi said: "The liar only lies out of self-contempt."

Al-Kurayzi recited these verses:

You lied! And whoever lies, his reward is

That he is not believed if he does not come with honesty,

If the liar is known for his lies, he will always be considered

By people like a liar, even when he tells the truth.

The Liar's Bane Occurs When Their Lies Are Forgotten

And if he is skillful, in the fact that we think he is enlightened.

The fact that lying degrades the individual in the eyes of his companions and that even if he tells the truth, they do not believe him, should be enough to make all humans firm on the truth.

The worst scourge of lying occurs when the liar's companion does not have a good memory, because this invites him to lie at any time and on every occasion.

Muhammad ibn 'Abdillah al-Baghdadi recited these verses to me:

If a man lacks these three things,

So even for a handful of dust, you must exchange him:

Integrity, truthfulness, and keeping

In his heart, hidden secrets.

Truthfulness elevates the person in this life and the next, just as lying degrades him in these two abodes.

If truthfulness had no other praiseworthy quality than that if a man is known for it, his lies are accepted as truth by those who hear them, then it would be obligatory on every intelligent person to strive to train his tongue until it becomes firm on the truth and far from falsehood.

Furthermore, being unable to express oneself is sometimes better than talking too much, because that is better than any words expressed inappropriately.

Chapter 6: Modesty

According to Abu Mas'ud al-Ansari (Allah be pleased with him), the Prophet (peace and blessings of Allah be upon him) said: Among the precepts that people retained from the first prophecies: if you have no modesty, do what you want.

The gifted with wisdom must constantly demonstrate modesty, because it constitutes the foundation of intelligence and the propagation of good.

Likewise, separating oneself from it constitutes the basis of ignorance and the propagation of vice.

Modesty is proof of intelligence, just as its absence is proof of ignorance.

Muhammad ibn 'Abdillah al-Baghdadi recited these verses to me:

If he lacks honor, he lacks modesty.

There is no good in one who lacks honor.

Preserve your modesty, because certainly

Only modesty is a mark of nobility.

Modesty is a word that refers to avoiding any detestable quality.

It is of two types:

· 1- The modesty and shame of the servant in relation to the performance of acts against which Allah, the Almighty, the Most Venerable, has warned him.

· 2- Shame and modesty in relation to performing acts and uttering words that creatures hate.

Both types are laudable, but one is obligatory, while the other is of secondary importance.

Thus, modesty regarding acts that Allah has forbidden is obligatory and modesty regarding acts that people hate is a plus.

If the person is endowed with modesty (haya), then the ingredients of goodness are present in him.

But if the immodest persists in his obscenity, then good is absent and vice is prevalent (in him).

Indeed, modesty constitutes an obstacle between the individual and the prohibited act.

Thus, strong modesty weakens the attraction to sins, while weak modesty strengthens desires.

The poet spoke the truth when he proclaimed these verses:

Nothing can stand between me and shameful acts

Except modesty, because it is a remedy against them

But if modesty goes away,

No more cure will be there.

The wise man must accustom himself to persisting in modesty among people.

The greatest reward of this act will be that he will accustom himself to praiseworthy qualities and avoid blameworthy acts.

Likewise, the greatest reward that Allah gives for modesty is deliverance from the Fire, (this reward a person gets) by persisting on it (having modesty) and abstaining from what Allah has forbidden.

The son of Adam was created endowed with both honor and vice in his relationship between Allah and himself and in his relationships with creatures.

If his modesty is strong, then his honor will be strong and his vice will be weakened.

If his modesty is weak, his vice will strengthen and his honor will weaken.

If a person's modesty is firm, their dignity will be preserved and their goodness will be recognized.

On the other hand, the one whose modesty leaves him will lose his happiness.

The one who loses his happiness becomes insignificant and hated by people.

He who is hated suffers, and he who suffers is depressed.

He who is depressed loses his reason, and he whose reason is affected, then most of his words will be against him instead of in his favor.

There is no remedy for the devoid of modesty and there is no modesty in the devoid of loyalty.

There is no loyalty in him who has no brothers, and he who has no modesty says and does whatever he wants.

Chapter 7: Humility

Narrated Abu Hurayrah (Allah be pleased with him), that the Messenger of Allah (peace and blessings of Allah be upon him) said: Charity in no way diminish the wealth (that a person has).

Allah only adds more honor to the servant who forgives.

Whoever is humble for Allah, He elevates his rank."

The intelligent must be humble and avoid arrogance.

If the only quality of humility was that it increased the rank of the person, this would be enough to make it obligatory to make it an adornment apart from anything else.

There are two types of humility: one praiseworthy and one blameworthy.

1- Laudable humility: it consists of refraining from acting with arrogance towards the servants of Allah or from feeling contempt for them.

2- Blameable humility: it consists of humbling oneself in the face of a person who owns a part of this world, out of desire for what they have.

The wise man must distance himself from any form of blameworthy humility and not move away, in any way, from praiseworthy humility.

Humility raises the rank of the individual and increases his benefits, as well as his nobility.

Humility for Allah is of two types:

· 1- The humility of the servant towards his Lord when he performs an act of obedience without marveling at his own works.

· This type of humility prevents him from being impressed by his own good deeds.

· 2- When the individual has little esteem for himself and looks at himself with contempt because of the sins he has committed, to the point that he believes that there is no one here on earth who accomplishes less of worship and more sins than him.

The intelligent avoids arrogance because of the detestable characteristics that it contains, such as the following:

- Looking down on others while being amazed by yourself and thinking that you are better than them.

- Despise people, because he who does not despise people does not look down on them.

- Compete with Allah, the Most High, in His Attributes, since greatness and magnificence are among the Attributes of Allah.

Therefore, anyone who seeks to rival Him in any of His Attributes will be thrown into the Fire unless He forgives them.

The poet spoke the truth when he recited:

Arrogance reduces intelligence and corrupts religion

It violates honor, so be careful!

Don't be greedy! Because certainly, in evil there is humiliation

And in forbearance there is honor, not in arrogance or ignorance, no!

Humility is accessible to everyone.

It brings peace, as well as harmony and repels resentment, as well as repulsion.

The fruit of humility is love and the fruit of contentment is comfort.

Humility increases the nobility of the noble, while arrogance increases the baseness of the base.

How arrogant can he be who was created from a drop of semen, who ends up as a decomposing body and who, between these two states, carries excrement within him?

Chapter 8: Good Living

According to Ibn Mas'ud (Allah be pleased with him), the Messenger of Allah (peace and blessings of Allah be upon him) said:

"Fire is forbidden to any accessible (the person who is close to people), gentle and simple (easygoing) person."

The wise man must show love to people by adopting good manners and abstaining from bad manners, because: "Good manners dispel sins as the sun melts ice and bad manners spoil good works like vinegar spoils honey."

It is possible for a person to have all the good manners, but for a single flaw to ruin them.

Endearing yourself to the people involves being cheerful, concise, gentle and forgiving, having good manners, being generous, and protecting against harm.

So whoever meets this description, those who love him will never be sad and those who are jealous of him will not be happy.

Indeed, the one whose joy is linked to the joy of others and who is close to people, regardless of who they are, deserves the best reward.

'Ali ibn Muhammad al-Bassami recited the following poem to me:

I am close to my community in every way possible,

By the best of what I have seen and have not seen.

I refrain from hideous features, whatever they may be

And I restrain myself from my desires and from being a liar.

The one who needs help from others when they love him is better than the one who needs no one but is hated.

The reason people don't like him is because he lacks good manners.

Indeed, the one who lacks good manners, his family and his neighbors will lose hope in him and will come to hate him.

His brothers will find him unbearable.

So much so that they will want to get rid of him and will hope for his downfall.

People hate an individual for different reasons, but the main one is that he commits sins forbidden by Allah.

Indeed, whoever exceeds the limits prescribed by Allah, angers Him and the angels.

Then, this anger is placed on Earth.

This is when almost everyone who encounters him finds him annoying and detestable.

It is obligatory for the right-thinking man to stay away from the characteristics that attract people's hatred towards him.

He must persist in acquiring the qualities that will lead people to love him.

The best way to become favorable with people and win their love is to willingly give of what you have in worldly things and to bear the evil you endure from them.

Chapter 9: Kindness

———

Jabir (Allah be pleased with him) reported that the Messenger of Allah (peace and blessings of Allah be upon him) said:

"Being good-natured (kind) with the people is charity."

The intelligent person must be kind to those he meets, without falling into flattery, since kindness is a charity towards a person, while flattery is a nuisance.

The kind person demonstrates affability, making the time spent in their company pleasant, without breaking the religious principles in any way.

So, when a person does not make an effort to behave well and begins to mix good manners with things that Allah hates, then he is showing flattery or deception, and not affability, because the end result is insignificant and futile.

The individual must persist in putting affability into practice, because it improves his affairs.

He who is not kind and pleasant to people, they get tired of him.

This is what Ali ibn Muhammad al-Bassami said in a poem:

Be kind to the impatient

He who is not kind to people, of him they will tire.

He who honors them is cherished by them,

As well as the one who is generous.

The wise man must show kindness to people like the man swimming in the direction of the current.

Whoever maintains relationships with people will make his life difficult and his love towards them can never be stable, because you can only achieve love by supporting them as they are, unless it involves sin.

In this case, there is no listening or obedience.

Humans are made up of different desires and natures.

So, as it is difficult for you to abandon what you naturally lean towards, it is complicated for others to do the same.

It is therefore not possible to feel sincere love for others except by living with them and accepting them as they are, as well as sometimes turning a blind eye to their transgressions.

'Ali (Allah be pleased with him) said: "Do not be two-faced, for this is a blameworthy character.

Be sincere to your brother when you advise him, whether it is pleasant or bitter.

Always support him and stay with him as long as he stays with you."

Chapter 10: Spreading the Greetings of Peace

According to Ibn Mas'ud (Allah be pleased with him), the Messenger of Allah (peace and blessings of Allah be upon him) said:

"'As-Salam' is one of the Names of Allah that He placed on earth, so spread salam among you.

If a Muslim passes by a group of people, greets them with the salam and they return the salute, then he has a degree of superiority over them by virtue of having mentioned the salam first.

If they don't return the salam, then someone better than them will answer."

The intelligent should spread the greeting of salam among the people, because he who greets the members of the community with salam receives the reward of freeing a slave.

The spread of salam is one of the causes of the disappearance of hidden hostility, bad humor and hatred.

It stops division and develops brotherhood.

'Ammar ibn Yasir said: "He who possesses the following three qualities possesses faith: almsgiving with little means, justice from one's self and striving to spread salam."

When the one gifted with wisdom meets his brother in Islam, he must greet him with salam and smile.

Whoever does this removes a bad deed from them both, just as a tree loses its leaves during the winter.

The individual attracts love when he meets the people around him with a cheerful face.

Al-Abrash recited the following verses to me:

Because of the beauty of his joy, the joyful brother is loved

And hatred is never absent in the one who frowns.

The miserliness of an individual, his dishonor will hasten

I have never seen a man who had to be more vigilant because of his generosity.

The smile is like food for the learned and breaks the heart of the wise, because joy extinguishes the fire of stubbornness and burns off anger.

It is a protection against the unjust and a security against the slanderer.

He who shows a happy face to people, they will never possess what he possesses without a generous benefactor.

The intelligent person blessed by good behavior does not need to frown at someone who does not react in the right way to his noble intention.

Rather, he should display happiness and joy, because perhaps Allah will bring this person back to the correct behavior for which it is obligatory to praise and thank Allah for guiding him, while He has prevented others to access it.

Hammad ibn Ishaq recited the following verses:

When you meet him, the young man is like water

He is charming, and what he offers is beautiful.

His smile makes you happy

And his face is radiant.

He is incapable of showing greed

Or any other vice.

His language is determined

And his eye is exhausted.

Habib ibn Abi Thabit said: "One of the forms of good behavior of a man is to smile while he talks with his friend."

Chapter 11: Joking

Anas (Allah be pleased with him) reports that the Prophet (peace and blessings of Allah be upon him) had a servant named Anjashah who had a beautiful voice.

The Prophet (peace and blessings of Allah be upon him) therefore said to him: O Anjashah, do not break the vessels of glasses.

The wise man must incline hearts towards him by (permissible praiseworthy) joking and refrain from scowling and looking severe.

The joke is of two types: laudable (praiseworthy or commendable) and blameworthy.

A commendable joke is one which is not tarnished by what Allah the Almighty hates and is not a sin or a cause of severance of kinship ties.

The blameworthy joke is one marked by hostility, which takes away beauty, destroys friendship, pushes the person to denigrate himself and makes the noble embittered.

Al-Rabi'ah said: "Beware of joking, for it can ruin a friendship and pierce the chest."

'Abdullah ibn Khabiq said: "Do not mock the honorable person, he will feel hatred towards you.

Don't make fun of the common person, they will become disrespectful towards you."

Muhammad ibn 'Abdillah recited the following verses to me:

Honor your companion, don't make hurtful jokes.

Of course, you see hatred through mockery.

How many jokes lead to close ties being severed?

Because of them, companions separated.

Joking for anything other than obedience to Allah takes away the beauty, ruins the friendships and generates bitterness and resentment.

The joke is called "mazah" in Arabic, derived from the word "zah" which means "to move away", because the joke implies moving away from the truth.

How many times have brothers argued and loved ones left each other because of something that started as a joke?

Joking can cause arguments from which the intelligent person must refrain.

Indeed, arguing is reprehensible in any situation and you can only be one of two people in an argument:

· 1- The one who is more learned than the other.

· In that case, why would you debate with someone less knowledgeable than you?

· 2- The one who is less learned than the other.

· In this case, how can you argue against someone more knowledgeable than you?

Mis'ar ibn Kidam said to his son Kidam:

Certainly Kidam, I offer you this sincere advice,

So my son, listen to what your father has to say.

Refrain from arguing and joking,

Because the friend does not like these two traits.

Despite my long experience, I have never recommended them

For a neighbor or close companion.

The young person, in the eyes of his own people, is belittled by ignorance

As well as in the eyes of people, irrespective of his lineage.

Muhammad ibn al-Munkadir said: My mother said to me when I was young: "Do not joke with the young man to the point of belittling him and making him act against you."

'Umar ibn al-Khattab (Allah be pleased with him) said: "He who laughs a lot lacks reverence and he who jokes a lot is not taken seriously.

He who does one thing very often is known for it."

Chapter 12: Solitude

———

According to Abu Sa'id al-Khudri (Allah be pleased with him), the Messenger of Allah (peace and blessings of Allah be upon him) was asked: O Messenger of Allah, what are the best actions?

He replied: "Jihad in the path of Allah."

He was asked: "And then?"

He said: "A man [who isolates himself] in the valley of a mountain, worshiping Allah and protecting people from his evil."

The wise person should generally withdraw from people and be cautious about their company.

Indeed, even if the only benefit of solitude was safety from sin, it would have been appropriate for the individual not to disturb his peace by insisting on something that could lead to an argument.

A large number of past scholars have used solitude in both its general and specific sense.

The reason for withdrawing from the whole world lies in what you already know about the way humans operate in hindering good and spreading evil.

They hide good and spread evil.

They accuse the scholar of being an innovator or a heretic and insult the ignorant.

They are jealous and envious of those above them.

They despise and disdain those below them.

They say that those who express themselves talk too much.

They say he who is silent is an idiot.

They treat the thrifty as a miser and the generous as a wasteful person.

Anyone who desires to be among such people and is deceived by people will eventually become remorseful.

Ibn Abi 'Ali said that Muhammad ibn Ya'qub al-'Abdi recited this poem to him:

If I say: here is a companion to whom I have pleased,

And he rejoiced in my person, so make an exchange for me.

Because I have never accompanied anyone

Without him betraying me or changing.

Makhul said: "Even though there is good in being around people, solitude is safer."

Ibrahim al-Bukhari said: I went to the Haram after Al-Maghrib and saw Fudayl sitting there.

So I approached, then sat near him.

He said: "Who is it?"

I replied: "Ibrahim."

He said: "What brings you here?"

I said, "I saw you alone, so I sat down with you."

He said, "Do you like to slander, deceive, or act like a hypocrite?"

I replied: "No."

He then said: "Leave me."

Chapter 13: Brotherhood

Anas (Allah be pleased with him) reports: The Messenger of Allah united in brotherhood Salman and Abu Al-Darda, as well as 'Awf ibn Malik and Al-Sa'b ibn Jathamah.

The wise man must be careful not to neglect the ties that unite him with his brothers and must prepare to share with them the ups and downs of life.

He who seeks comfort from his brother in times of distress and sadness, his spirit will be better able to fight depression and push it away.

Muhammad ibn 'Imran Al-Dabbi recited this poem:

A man without his brothers, how can we describe him?

The hand is grasped by the wrist

The cut one is therefore of no use

Just like the mutilated arm.

The wise should not consider as a brother anyone who does not assist him during difficult times and does not participate in his good times.

A brother in fellowship can be better than a brother by blood.

The best way to preserve fraternal bonds is to show consideration to the affairs of those who love him.

True love between brothers is that which is not based on profit nor is it damaged by refusal.

Love is peace just as hatred is fear.

The wise man should know that the purpose of fellowship is not to meet together and eat and drink.

Even the donkey and the mule eat and drink together.

Thieves come together to commit crimes, without the love between them increasing.

Rather, some of the things that bring about brotherhood are measured gait, low voice, absence of excessive admiration, humility, and refraining from arguments.

A man should not overwhelm his brothers with gifts and provisions so much so that he gets tired of them, because if the child sucks for too long, the mother can become exasperated and put him aside.

It is not appropriate to refuse to meet the need of your brother, forcing him into adversity and being satisfied with his difficulty.

The intelligent must not take a bad person as a brother, because the vicious are like deadly snakes: they contain only bites and poisons.

When the vile individual fraternizes, he brings resentment and fear.

On the other hand, the noble and generous person is loved from the first meeting, even if we never see him again.

Yunus ibn 'Ubayd was afflicted by a great difficulty.

Someone then said to him: "Didn't Ibn 'Awf visit you? ".

He then replied: "When we trust in the love of our brother, we are not hurt that he does not visit us."

The wise man should try not to be harsh with his brothers.

He must strive to abolish his aggressiveness if it arises in him.

He must not regard harshness lightly, whatever it may be, even the slightest, because when we consider a thing to be tiny, it quickly assembles until it becomes immense.

Rather, he must do his best to eliminate it, because there is no point in being honest without respect and no point in understanding without piety.

Among the most ignorant of men is he who associates with his brothers without fulfilling their rights and who seeks reward in ostentation.

There is nothing more vain than love given to someone who is not worth it and a good deed done to the ungrateful.

Chapter 14: Avoiding Conflict

According to Abu Al-Darda (Allah be pleased with him), the Prophet (peace and blessings of Allah be upon him) said: The first things my Lord forbade me after worshiping idols were cursing donkeys and arguing with men."

The wise man must know that those who love him will never be jealous of him and those who are not jealous of him will never be enemies.

Avoiding conflict in all its forms is better for the intelligent than going through it.

Mahdi ibn Sabiq recited the following poem:

The number of your brothers, try to increase

For they are pillars in need, as well as purification.

A thousand close friends are not too many for a companion,

Whereas with just one enemy you are already in excess.

The wise man must not respond to evil in the same way or use insult and slander as weapons against his enemy, because using his faults and pointing out his faults only exposes their author to the same thing.

The intelligent does not spare those who fear him and takes note of the weaknesses of his enemy while refraining from slandering him.

The wise man does not weaken his enemy by subterfuge and trickery, because seeking to weaken the enemy in this way is deception and he who deceives is not safe from being deceived.

This is the case except if the enemy is of modest condition and means.

The individual must show forbearance and patience towards such a person, for the lowly enemy deserves clemency, just as the frightened who seeks protection deserves to be given refuge.

Having an intelligent individual as an enemy is better than shaking hands with the ignorant.

Ahmad ibn Muhammad al-Bakri recited these verses to me:

It's better to have an intelligent enemy

Than having an ignorant friend.

So, spare yourself from having the ignorant as a friend,

Because the friend is the witness of his friend.

The wise man considers each step before moving forward, then he gets close enough to his enemy to understand what he needs, but he does not get too close or risk being reckless.

The person gifted with reason does not take enemies when it is possible to be allies.

He does not take as enemies those he cannot avoid nor those against whom he cannot defend himself except by flight.

The best strategy for defeating an enemy is to get them to let their guard down, show them that you don't take them as an enemy, and befriend their friends.

However, hostility after friendship is a huge abomination that does not come from the wise person.

So whoever leans towards this must always leave himself space to rectify himself.

The wise man does not let the faults and bad character traits that his enemy attributes to him change him.

Indeed, these things are not true, no matter how much one's enemy insists.

He cannot know rest while his enemy remains, just as the sick cannot know the pleasure of sleep and food until he recovers.

According to Abu Musa (Allah be pleased with him), the Prophet (peace and blessings of Allah be upon him) said: The example of a good companion is like the perfume seller: even if you don't get his pleasant scent, you can at least smell it.

The example of the bad companion is like the blacksmith: even if you are not burned by his fire, the sparks will reach you.

The wise man persists in associating with good people and staying away from bad people.

Indeed, good people are quick to form relationships and slow to break them.

On the other hand, bad people are quick to break off relationships and slow to form them.

Hanging around bad people leads good people to think bad thoughts about people.

Anyone who makes friends with them is not safe from becoming one of them.

Therefore, the wise man must stay away from suspicious individuals, so that people do not have suspicious thoughts about him.

Muhammad ibn 'Abdillah ibn Zinji al-Baghdadi recited these verses to me:

It is up to you to be the brother of the determined,

Because there are few of them, so join them

Instead of those you frequented,

Honor your person and try to preserve it,

Because when you have frequented the vilest people

Your anger will be aroused.

Malik ibn Dinar said: "It is better to push rocks with good people than to enjoy dessert with bad people."

The wise man neither sullies his honor nor accustoms himself to the causes that lead to evil by associating with evil people.

He also does not neglect to preserve his honor and improve his spirituality through association with good people.

It's better to spend time with a dog than with someone who doesn't do anything good.

Anyone who associates with a bad person is not safe, in the same way that someone who enters a place known for its vice will be viewed suspiciously.

The poet Mansur ibn Muhammad al-Kurayzi said:

And even if he displays the good, his vice is not far away

With a bad person once, I knew good

And if there was neither good nor evil in him

I would have rejoiced at the reward on the scales

But it is bad and contains no quality

He has no vice if he is endowed with patience.

The wise should seek refuge with Allah from the companion who brings no good when Allah is mentioned and who, when Allah is forgotten, does not bring Him to mind.

The one who keeps bad company is just as bad.

Just as good people only associate with the pious, bad people only accompany the vile.

Abd Al-Wahid ibn Zayd said: "Sit with the people of religion here below (in this world), for they do not indulge in evil words when they come together."

Sahl ibn Sa'd reports that the Messenger of Allah (peace and blessings of Allah be upon him) said: There is no good in associating with someone who does not recognize your rights as you recognize his.

If Allah grants an individual the blessing of sincere friendship with a good Muslim, he must protect it and hold on to it.

He must prepare to reconnect with his friend if he breaks up with him, to approach him if he turns away, to spend time with him if he avoids him and to invite him if he moves away.

This until these traits become pillars of his character.

Indeed, one of the worst faults is to be unstable in friendship.

Al-Muntasr ibn Bilal al-Ansari recited the following verses to me:

For how many friends, friendship

Is only installed on their languages

They will have stabbed you in the back

Without feeling any regrets.

The wise man does not befriend the lunatic or display affection without feeling it in his heart.

What he feels is always greater than what he shows.

He will do this during difficult times and pleasant times, because fraternity is not praiseworthy if it is unstable.

A man from Khuza'ah wrote the following verses:

My brother is not the one who shows me his love

Only by velvet words

Rather, my brother is the one who has always loved

Even in times of difficulty

Whose property is mine if I am destitute

And everything that belongs to me is his if my destiny varies

Fraternity is not glorious in ease

Indeed, if you deny your brother in difficulty

So it's just a "How are you?"

Or a "Welcome",

But with his money he will be cunning

Like a wise fox.

One of the best signs of the sincerity of a person's love or affection is in the eyes.

Indeed, the eyes cannot hide what is in the heart.

Therefore, the wise judge the sincerity of a person by his heart and by the eyes of his brother.

According to Abu Hurayrah, the Prophet (peace and blessings of Allah be upon him) said: A man visited one of his brothers who lived in another village.

Allah sent an Angel on his way.

When he arrived, Angel asked him: "Where are you going?"

He replied: "I am going to visit a brother who lives in this village."

The angel said: "Have you entrusted him with anything that you would like to ensure is in good condition?"

The man said: "No, except that I love him for Allah," the man replied.

The Angel then said to him: "I have been sent to you from Allah to tell you that Allah has loved you as you have loved this person for Him (for His sake)."

The wise man should visit his brothers regularly and be concerned about their condition.

The visitor must look for two results:

- The future reward

- The joy of being in the company of his brother.

Al-Faryabi said: Waki' visited me from Bayt Al-Maqdis and was in the state of ihram for 'Umrah.

He said to me: "Abu Muhammad, you were not on my way, but I wanted to visit you and stay in your company."

So he stayed with me for one night.

Then, Ibn al-Mubarak visited me and also entered the state of ihram for 'Umrah from Bayt Al-Maqdis.

He stayed with me for three days.

I told him: "Abu 'Abd Al-Rahman, ten days remain."

He replied: "No, the hospitality is for three days only."

Visitors are of two types:

· 1- He who seeks to improve his own person and that of his brother by ridding him of the defects and errors present in him.

· Frequent visits from this type of visitor are appreciated, as they do not lead to boredom.

· They rather lead to friendship and closeness.

————————

· 2- THE ONE WITH WHOM love never takes root between him and his brother.

· His visits do not lead to the disappearance of the discomfort between them.

· It is best that visits from this type of visitor are limited, because if they are frequent they will only lead to boredom and resentment.

· Indeed, what is given in too large a quantity is unpleasant and what is rare is desirable.

· In reality, many ahadith have been attributed to the Prophet (peace and blessings of Allah be upon him) clearly calling into question the incessant visits, such as this one:

· "Occasional visits increase love."

He who maintains good relations with his brothers does not need to visit them often, because love is deeply rooted.

If, however, the relationship is damaged by a lack of visits, it is because the love was superficial.

As for the one who has not developed relationships with his brothers, then it is better for him to refrain from frequent visits so as not to become a painful burden.

According to Anas ibn Malik (Allah be pleased with him), the Prophet (peace and blessings of Allah be upon him) said: The example of a good companion is like the perfume seller: even if you don't get his pleasant scent, you can at least smell it.

The example of the bad companion is like the blacksmith: even if you are not burned by his fire, the sparks will reach you.

The sensible man should not waste his time with fools.

Rather, he should spend time with intelligent and wise people, because even if you do not receive a part of their intelligence, you will receive the same esteem that they enjoy.

As for the idiot, even if he does not harm you with his ignorance, you will be criticized for having associated with him.

If the wise person does not know the signs that allow one to recognize the ignorant, here are some of them: hasty answering questions, lack of verification, excessive laughter, constantly looking around, slander from good people and association with bad people.

They do not know him and are saddened when you avoid him, but if you turn to him, he will deceive you.

If you are nice to him, he ignores you, but if you ignore him, he is nice to you.

If you harm him, he will be good to you, but if you are good to him, he will harm you.

If you oppress him, he will treat you fairly, but if you are just to him, he will be unjust to you.

Among the ignorant are those whose characters are not calmed by the calm of others.

They neither hide their faults nor benefit from turning a blind eye to their faults.

The wise should not associate with this type of people, because they become impudent with those who associate with them.

Don't you see that the people of Sudan are not particularly brave, and yet they show boldness with lions because of their familiarity with them?

Indeed, the character of the gifted with wisdom includes gentleness, restraint, level-headedness, calmness, being trustworthy, generosity, wisdom, knowledge, piety, fairness, strength, determination, politeness, clairvoyance, good tolerance, humility, indulgence, and beneficence.

Therefore, he who has received the benefit of friendship from a wise person must attach his hand to his and never leave him, whatever happens.

As for the wise, he should not associate with someone from whom it is impossible to benefit.

According to Abu Hurayrah, the Prophet (peace and blessings of Allah be upon him) said: Beware of suspicion, because suspicion is certainly the most false of words.

Do not spy, do not seek to discover the faults of others, do not hate each other, be servants of Allah and brothers to one another!"

The wise man must hold on to his integrity by avoiding spying on others and looking for their faults.

He must take care of rectifying his own mistakes.

He who focuses on his own faults instead of those of others nourishes the serenity of his heart.

He never tires, for whenever an individual discovers a deficiency in his own character, he need only discover a similar thing in his brother.

Those who focus on the faults of their brothers lead their hearts to be blinded.

Their bodies get tired and they make excuses for their own faults.

The weakest of people is the one who criticizes others because of their faults.

The one who is even weaker than him criticizes people for faults that he himself possesses.

He who criticizes people is criticized by people.

Al-Kurayzi recited the following poem to me:

Everyone sees the faults of others

But he is blinded by his own faults.

What good is there in him

Who doesn't see his faults

But for whom the faults of his close friend

Are crystal clear?

Spying is a branch of hypocrisy, just as the good opinion of people is a branch of faith.

The wise man has a good opinion of his brothers and takes into account his own misfortunes and problems.

The ignorant does not trust his brothers and does not think of his crimes and his reproaches.

Distrust is of two types:

· 1- The first is prohibited by the judgment of the Prophet (peace and blessings of Allah be upon him).

· 2- The second is recommended.

Forbidden distrust is general distrust of all Muslims, as previously explained.

The recommended distrust is that of those who display hostility and resentment towards you for religious or worldly reasons.

It is also about that towards the one whose betrayal or trickery you have reason to fear.

In this case, it is important to be wary of his stratagems and deception, so that he does not take advantage of your inattention and dominate you.

Al-Abrash told me the following verses on this subject:

Thinking well of people is good in appropriate situations,

But regret can, in the end, ambush you after hiding.

Distrust makes the face loathsome,

But its ugliness can sometimes be a protection.

The sagacious man must distinguish himself from rude people by his manners and his actions by staying away from looking for the faults of others.

Indeed, he who seeks people's secrets will find his own secrets being sought.

However, it may be that his secrets are greater than those he seeks to discover in others.

Furthermore, how can it be appropriate for the Muslim to criticize another Muslim for faults that he himself possesses?

The daughter of 'Abdullah ibn Muti' al-Aswad said to her husband Talha ibn 'Abdillah ibn 'Awf: "O Talhah, I do not know anyone worse than your companions."

He replied: "Show restraint, don't say that about them! What have you seen from them to speak like this?"

She replied: "When you are well, they are with you, but when you are going through difficulties, they abandon you."

He said, "You just described their good manners."

She said, "How is that good manners?!"

He says: "They accompany us in times of strength, when we can bear them, and leave us alone in times of weakness, when we cannot bear their company."

Chapter 20: Channeling your Desires

According to Anas (Allah be pleased with him), the Prophet (peace and blessings of Allah be upon him) said: The son of Adam grows old, but two things remain young in him: desire and jealousy.

Allah the Most High created humans with a desire and inclination towards this fleeting world so as not to spoil it, for it is the abode of the righteous, a source of income for the pious, a place that contains sustenance for believers and provisions for good doers.

So, if people were devoid of desire for this material world, it would be abandoned and fall into ruin.

Then, no one would find a way to feed themselves to help them fulfill the obligations that Allah has imposed on them, let alone the additional rewards in the afterlife earned through supererogatory acts.

On the other hand, excessive desire is blameworthy.

Muhammad ibn Nasr al-Madini recited the following poem to me:

O you who possess so much desire

Occupied by a world that won't last

I have never seen a more vile desire

Than towards the wealth to be amassed.

No ! But the decree comes from Allah

To become weak and ruined.

You know the truth, but

You don't think the truth to be incumbent.

Desire does not increase wealth.

The worst thing that can befall the greedy person is that because of his desire he becomes incapable of enjoying the fruits of his labor.

He then tires himself searching for something he may never attain before death meets him.

If the greedy would avoid being excessive in his desire and rely on the Creator of heaven, then the Lord, the Protector, the Almighty, the Noble, would surround him with that which he did not even pursue and with a success that he would never have achieved by his greedy pursuit.

Desire is the sign of need just as avarice is the garment of poverty.

Greed is the seed of desire, just as pride is the seed of ignorance.

Stinginess is the sister of desire, just as condescension is the twin of insolence.

There is no rest for him who obeys his desires towards this world.

He will be condemned in this life and in the next.

Instead, the individual's intention should be towards fulfilling Allah's obligations.

His desires must have limits that must not be crossed, because if his goal has no limit or conclusion, it will harm his person and exhaust his body.

Desire that is limited, without being excessive, endowed with an accessible objective, is the laudable desire.

Chapter 21: Repelling Jealousy

According to Abu Hurayrah (Allah be pleased with him), the Prophet (peace and blessings of Allah be upon him) said: Don't hate each other, don't be jealous of each other, don't argue.

Be servants of Allah and brothers!

The sensible man must avoid jealousy at all times.

Indeed, the worst aspect of jealousy is being dissatisfied with Allah's decree and wishing the opposite of what Allah has decided for His servants.

In addition to this, the jealous person wants the benefits of another Muslim to disappear.

The soul of the jealous person finds no rest until he sees his brother's blessing disappear.

If the wise man feels jealous towards his brother, he should do his best to hide this feeling and not let it show to others.

Jealousy mainly occurs between people who are similar in ethnicity or social rank.

Man does not achieve any position or status in this world without meeting someone who hates him for that or is jealous of him.

The jealous person is an obstinate adversary.

The wise should therefore not take him as arbiter in a trial, the jealous will judge against him.

If he is angry with someone, he will be angry with him.

If he steals something, he will steal from him.

If he gives, it will be to someone else.

If he holds back, it will be against him.

If he stops anyone, it will be him.

He will consider the benefit received by the one he is jealous of as a grave sin or crime.

A man must therefore be cautious towards those who are of the same ethnic group as him, his peers, his neighbors and his cousins.

A man said to Shabib ibn Shayabbah: "Of course, I love you very much."

He replied: "You spoke the truth."

The man asked, "How do you know?"

He replied: "For you are neither a neighbor nor a cousin."

The wise and prudent individual must resign himself to bearing the pain of the jealousy of others.

Those who will be the most jealous of him will be his neighbors and brothers if they are not invested in religion, his friends then his relatives, because in reality, relatives are in the image of scorpions, except those whom Allah has preserved and kept away from harmful people who have not chosen to take the path of the wise and do not desire the position of the people of understanding in matters of following religion.

Rather, they desire the opposite of that.

Jealousy leads to unhappiness.

Have you not seen Iblis? He was jealous of Adam, his jealousy therefore caused his misfortune.

He was cursed after being respected.

It is easy to please anyone in this world except the jealous person, because he will only be happy when the person loses the benefit that made him jealous.

Chapter 22: Don't Get Angry

According to Abu Hurayrah or Jabir (may Allah be pleased with them), a man said to the Messenger of Allah (peace and blessings of Allah be upon him): Teach me something that isn't too heavy for me so I can hold on to it."

The Prophet (peace and blessings of Allah be upon him) replied: "Do not get angry."

The most reasonable people are those who don't get angry.

The ones who have the most thoughtful responses are the ones who don't get upset.

Anger is more harmful to the wise than fire is to the dry bush.

Indeed, when a person becomes angry, he loses his intelligence and common sense, and therefore says: "I allowed anger to have control over me and I did something that hurt me and has disgraced me and brought my own destruction."

Al-Kurayzi recited the following verses to me:

I see no good apart from good character,

And I don't see intellect to be right except through good manners,

And I saw no enemy that I tested,

To be more hostile than the anger towards the reason (intellect) of an angry man.

Anger is one of the characteristics of the ignorant, while composure is the adornment of the wise.

Anger sows the seeds of regret.

So, it is better for the individual to correct what made them angry before they get angry, rather than after.

Bukar ibn Muhammad said: Ibn 'Awn never gets angry.

If someone tries to annoy him, he says, "May Allah bless you."

Muhammad ibn Ishaq ibn Habib al-Wasiti narrated to me these verses:

People never ate food

Gentler and with a more praiseworthy outcome than anger.

However, man cannot have an adornment,

More splendid and radiant than religion and good manners.

The wise person who confronts that which opposes what his soul desires must remind himself of the frequency of his sins and the continual mercy of Allah.

Thus, his anger will subside.

If anger had no other blameworthy characteristic than the fact that all judges without exception agree on the absence of good judgment in the angry person, that would have been enough to avoid it at all costs.

Furthermore, no one accepts anger as an excuse for pronunciation of divorce or emancipation but some jurists accept the drunken (intoxication) excuse in both situations.

So consider this.

Humans are naturally predisposed to both anger and patience.

Therefore, one who is both angry and patient is not blameworthy as long as his anger does not lead him to say or do something hateful.

However, it is better to abandon it completely.

'Abd Al-Malik ibn Marwan said: "The man who does not get angry is not patient, because the individual learns true patience only in times of anger."

According to Sahl ibn Sa'd (Allah be pleased with him), a man asked the Prophet (peace and blessings of Allah be upon him): O Messenger of Allah, teach me something for which Allah will love me and people will love me.

He replied: "Abstain from this world and Allah will love you.

Abstain from what people have and they will love you."

The sensible man must completely renounce the desire for the goods of others.

Indeed, to hope for something that you are sure of is indigence, what then of hoping for something that you are not sure of obtaining?

The one who proclaimed the following verses spoke the truth:

I will offer despair the means by which it reaches me:

As long as I count on you, I will have to resign myself to living in suffering.

But I will be patient

A determination by which I would achieve

The Pleasure of Allah and the Closeness of People

The soul is satisfied and the world is big

The home includes the couple and the single person.

The noblest form of wealth is that of one who has no need of others or what they possess.

Indeed, there is no wealth in need.

He who restrains himself will reach the pinnacle of wealth.

Blessed is the individual whose heart is reluctant and whose gaze is never affected by desire.

He who wishes to be free must never desire what he does not possess, for desire is poverty and the renunciation of desire is wealth.

He who desires wealth is humiliated and submissive.

On the other hand, he who is satisfied with what he has is moderate and rich.

The wise man refrains from coveting the possessions of his friends, because this is humiliating.

He renounces those of his enemies, because it is a safe refuge whose abandonment is destruction.

Renouncing material possessions brings peace and determination.

The thirst for goods brings worry and humiliation.

How many greedy people have burned out, been humiliated and never achieved their goals?

How many people who are satisfied with what they have are peaceful and lead productive lives, achieving their dreams and much more.

Zubayr ibn al-'Awwam (Allah be pleased with him) reports that the Prophet (peace and blessings of Allah be upon him) said: The fact that one of you takes a rope and goes to the mountain to bring back a bundle of wood on his back and sells it so that Allah spares him the humiliation of begging is better for him than stretching his hand to people that they give to him or refuse to give to him.

The wise must always refrain from begging, because resigning oneself to begging leads to degradation, while the determination not to beg leads to strength, honor and elevation in rank.

The man of wisdom does not ask anything from people for which they would reject him and does not beg from them for anything that they would forbid him.

He must hold on to his abstinence, as well as his honor, and not seek to obtain something on one side while neglecting that thing on the other.

It is better to miss a need than to try to fill it with the help of the wrong person.

Indeed, when you ask for help from someone who does not deserve it, you lower yourself two levels and you elevate the person you ask to a level higher than the one he deserves.

Sufyan ibn 'Uyaynah said: "He who asks for help from the vile person will have elevated him above his true rank."

Among the worst disasters is having bad offspring and begging.

Worrying about asking for help is half of decay.

So what can we say about the one who rushes to begging?

The strong and determined do not give importance to this world.

They abstain from the possessions of others and pass over what is offered to them.

Asking for charity from your brothers in Islam leads to anguish and receiving charity from others and the opposite of gift.

The wise should not sacrifice his honor to someone who respects and recognizes him.

What then can we say about the one who doesn't even take the time to respond to him and who doesn't respect him?

The last encounter is with death, but worse than that is being weighed down by the burden of begging.

Indeed, if begging succeeds in making the need disappear, the humiliation remains.

On the other hand, if it fails, the individual is subjected to two humiliations: that of having asked and that of having been rejected.

Chapter 25: Contentment

Ibn 'Umar (Allah be pleased with him) reports: The Messenger of Allah (peace and blessings of Allah be upon him) took me by the shoulder and said to me: Be in this world like a stranger or a traveler.

The Prophet (peace and blessings of Allah be upon him) ordered Ibn 'Umar in this hadith to be in the image of the foreigner or the traveler.

It is as if he had ordered him to exercise moderation and frugality.

Indeed, the foreigner and the traveler do not expect to live in opulence and luxury during their absence.

Rather, it is frugality that is most likely to appear.

'Ali ibn Muhammad al-Bassami recited these verses to me:

Among the best forms of sustenance is that which calms

The eye of the blessed, rich or poor.

Finding happiness in a small amount

Is better for you than wealth in the middle of a lush garden.

One of the greatest and most important gifts that Allah can give to His servant is contentment.

There is nothing more soothing for the body than being satisfied with the decree of Allah.

If contentment had no other laudable characteristic than appeasement and preventing one from falling into bad situations, that would be enough to make it obligatory for the wise in every situation.

Muhammad ibn Ishaq al-Wasiti recited this poem to me:

Praises to Allah always and for eternity

People have been clothed in shame and greed

There is no beauty except in the one who is satisfied with a small amount

Certainly! Contentment is the adornment of religion and dignity.

The man gifted with reason knows that he (being a human) will not satisfied with what he possesses (even if he possesses a lot), and for someone whithout contentment, wealth will not remove his need for more.

Indeed, his possessions will not satisfy his need for more and more.

So, the one who knows how to control himself will be happy and more satisfied than the one who has a fortune.

The wise man takes his revenge on greed through contentment, just as he would seek protection from an enemy through punishment.

Indeed, the thing that preserves the wise from food and wealth is the same as that which grants the ignorant food and wealth.

A man from the Khuza'ah said in the following poem:

I saw the rich and the poor divided into two categories,

The deceiver was deprived and the weak took advantage

He persists, exhausted, nothing benefits,

And the comfortable, the rested, benefits.

Contentment is found in the heart.

So he whose heart is free from desires and wishes, his hands will also be free from desires and wishes.

On the other hand, he whose heart is filled with needs, his goods will be of no benefit to him.

He who is blessed with contentment is never touched by bitterness.

He leads a safe and peaceful life.

As for the one who is deprived of contentment, his desires, his efforts and his frustration for what he thinks he has missed know no bounds.

'Abdullah ibn 'Amr ibn al-'As (Allah be pleased with him) reports: I heard the Messenger of Allah (peace and blessings of Allah be upon him) say: Allah wrote the destinies of creatures 500 years before creating the heavens and the earth.

The wise must place his trust in the One who is responsible for the provision of sustenance.

Trust in Allah is the structure of faith, the companion of monotheism.

It is the cause which leads to the negation of poverty and the presence of peace.

He who has a sound heart will not place his (true) trust in Allah, the Almighty, the Noble, until (and unless) he trusts in Allah and what He has with Him more than to anything else.

Whoever puts his trust in Allah, He will make him independent of people and provide him with sustenance from countless sources.

Abu Al-Darda said: "Sustenance seeks the servant just as he seeks it."

'Abd al-Aziz ibn Sulayman al-Abrash recited the following poem to me:

If, within an immense immobile rock

Shaped by Allah in the middle of the ocean,

If there was sustenance for the servant, he would have opened himself,

And everything it contains would have gone towards him.

Or if his path lay beneath the seven lands,

Allah would have facilitated its ascension

Until he reaches what is written for him in the Table.

So either it (sustenance) will come to him or he will go to it.

The wise know that the powerless achieve what they need through a mixture of prudence and benefit.

He therefore does not get angry about what he cannot obtain nor about what he is certain to have, because this lower world (the world and what it contains) comes to the individual without any difficulty.

He who is deprived of something will not attain it, even if he seeks it.

He who is granted something will obtain it even without moving.

Trust in Allah cuts the heart from connections by rejecting creatures and tying itself with need to the One who changes situations.

It is possible for a man to be rich and prosperous while being sincere in his trust in Allah.

This happens when he doesn't care whether he has what he has or not.

When he is prosperous, he is grateful.

When he has little, he is satisfied.

It is also possible that a person who has nothing does not place his trust in Allah. This happens if he prefers wealth to poverty, is not satisfied when he is poor and not grateful when he is rich.

Al-Kurayzi proclaimed the following verses to me:

If this world were obtained by excellent reasoning

I would have reached the highest degree,

But sustenance is a share and a distribution

Of the wealth of the Owner, and is not obtained by the trickeries of those who run after it.

Chapter 27: Patience

According to Ibn 'Abbas, the Messenger of Allah (peace and blessings of Allah be upon him) said: The first thing that Allah created was the Pen.

Then, He ordered it to write down everything that will happen until the Day of Resurrection."

The wise man must be certain that everything will end.

There are some things that will inevitably happen and some things that will never happen.

The creatures have no way of changing this.

So, when times are tough, you need to surround yourself with a lower garment that has two ends: patience and acceptance.

This is with the aim of receiving the full reward for this action.

How many times has it seemed like the whole world was affected by a calamity only to find ease following?

Al-Muntasr ibn Bilal al-Ansari recited the following poem to me:

It could be that Allah brings him joy

Every day of his life,

Or it might not prevail,

Or that you see him rejoicing over a trial that has assailed him.

If the test intensifies, then expect its finality,

For Allah has decreed that difficulty will be followed by ease.

The person gifted with reason must try to remain patient when a challenge appears, because if he succeeds, his patience will elevate him to the level of acceptance and satisfaction.

He who does not have patience must make efforts to learn (acquire) it, because it is the first step towards satisfaction and happiness.

If patience were a person, it would be noble and generous, because patience is the source of good and constitutes the basis of piety.

Patience is a structure for tolerance, an aid for intelligence, a propagation of good and a path for those who are lost.

The first level is worry, then caution, then certainty, then tolerance, then patience, then satisfaction which constitutes the last level.

Maymun ibn Mahran said: "Without patience, the servant will not obtain any share of the immense amount of good coming from the Prophet (peace and blessings of Allah be upon him) or anyone else."

Al-Ghalabi recited the following poem:

Certainly, I immediately saw the good in patience,

And it suffices to say that through it you achieve many rewards.

You must obey Allah in every situation,

Because if you do it, you will have full compensation.

Patience is of three types:

· - Patience in the face of sins

· - Patience in obedience

· - Patience in the face of trials.

The wise man behaves with prudence in these three situations through patience and the crossing of the degrees that we mentioned previously.

This until he rises to the level of satisfaction with the decree of Allah, the Almighty, the Noble, in times of trial and ease.

I ask Allah to raise me to this level by His grace.

Chapter 28: Forgiveness

Abu Hurayrah (Allah be pleased with him) reports that a man came to the Prophet (peace and blessings of Allah be upon him) and said to him: O Messenger of Allah! I have relatives with whom I maintain family ties, but they break them, I am good to them, but they harm me, I am lenient towards them, but they are rude to me.

The Prophet (peace and blessings of Allah be upon him) replied:

"If it is as you say, it is as if you were making them eat hot coals, and Allah will not cease to give you the upper hand over them as long as you act in this way."

The wise man must mentally prepare himself to forgive people and not seek retribution in the face of mistreatment.

There is indeed nothing better than beneficence to stop mistreatment and there is nothing that causes even more mistreatment than reacting with similar behavior.

Mansur ibn Muhammad al-Kurazi recited the following verses to me:

I will command myself to forgive every person who has offended me,

Even if they commit many wrongdoings against me,

Because there are only three types of people: the honorable, the one who is well treated

And the one who seeks revenge.

As for him who is above me, I know his merit,

So I am in the truth and the truth is what follows.

As for the one below me, he says my honor is safe

Through his response, even though people criticized.

As for the one who is like me, if he was wrong

Indulgence dictates the actions of the noble, so with kindness I

would treat.

He who desires abundant reward, pure devotion and to be mentioned well must tolerate the weight of destruction and swallow the bitterness of fighting against his desires using the Sunnah we have mentioned about maintaining relationships when they are broken: generosity in the face of avarice, gentleness in the face of harshness and forgiveness in the face of injustice.

This, because these are the best behaviors of the inhabitants of the heavens and the earth.

The wise man must persist in forgiveness and forbearance even when he is mistreated by the whole world, hoping in this for Allah's forgiveness for his own misdeeds that he has committed throughout his life.

Indeed, those who forgive are rewarded and those who choose to take revenge, even if they succeed, end up in regret.

'Ali ibn Muhammad al-Bassami recited the following poem to me:

If you never overlook your brother's mistakes,

So tomorrow you won't pass over mine,

And how can the stranger expect you to help him

If your goodness is too weak to help your friend?

The people who are freest from resentment and malice are those who are above revenge.

The best people are those who oppose indulgence to ignorance and who is better than the one who responds to mistreatment with beneficence?

As for responding to good with good, it is only a reciprocity in behavior that even animals sometimes apply.

If forgiveness and refraining from mistreating people contained no benefits other than inner peace and good temperament, the wise man would still not waste his time behaving like an animal by responding to evil with the evil.

He who acts evil in response to evil is evil, even if he is not the one who started it.

Chapter 29: Nobility

Abu Hurayrah (Allah be pleased with him) reports that the Prophet (peace and blessings of Allah be upon him) was asked: O Messenger of Allah! Who is the noblest of people?

The Prophet (peace and blessings of Allah be upon him) replied: He among them who has the most piety.

[The people] said: That's not what we're questioning you about.

The Prophet (peace and blessings of Allah be upon him) said: It is Joseph, the messenger of Allah, son of the messenger of Allah, son of the messenger of Allah, son of the close friend of Allah.

[The people] said: That's not what we're questioning you about.

The Prophet (peace and blessings of Allah be upon him) said: Are you asking me about the Arab tribes?"

[The people] replied: "Yes.

The Prophet (peace and blessings of Allah be upon him) said: The best of them before Islam are the best of them in Islam when they understand it.

The noblest of people is the one who fears Allah and the noble person is the pious person.

Piety (Taqwa) corresponds to the determination to fulfill obligations and to stay away from prohibitions.

So the one that perfects these two characteristics, he deserves to be described as noble.

Anyone who regresses in these two traits or in one of them or in one of their branches will have reduced his nobility proportionally.

Zayd ibn Thabit said: "There are three traits found only in the noble: neat appearance, tolerance of mistakes and patience."

Ibn Zinji al-Baghdadi recited the following poem:

I have seen the truth that the nobles know

For his friend and the contemptible have denied

That if a young man is good and noble,

So all his actions are noble and of quality.

The noble is not malicious, envious, unjust, thoughtless, careless, insolent, arrogant, dishonest or impatient.

He does not break off relationships, does not harm his brothers, and does not neglect his duties.

The noble is generous in friendship: he gives even when nothing is asked of him and protects others even when they are not afraid.

He moves away from power and maintains family ties.

The noble is gentle when compassion is needed, while the ignoble are harsh even when treated with kindness.

The noble admires the noble, but does not denigrate the base, does not harm the wise, does not mock the fool, and does not associate with the evildoer.

His brothers are important to him.

If he knows they want something, he graciously spends on them.

He never transforms friendship and love into agonizing hostility.

If we offer him fraternity, he never breaks it for anything.

The noble brings about laudable effects in this life and pleasant works in the next.

He is loved by all, by those near and far, by the bitter and the contented.

Enemies and critics move away from him.

The wise and the noble accompany him.

I have seen nothing that diminishes honor more than poverty, whether it is poverty of heart or of goods.

Al-Muntasr ibn Bilal al-Ansari recited the following verses:

Certainly ! Wealth will indeed make the young man

Distracted and poverty will degrade the man

And by money, the poor man was raised

And nothing demeans the noble soul like poverty.

Chapter 30: Don't Listen to the Slanderer

According to Hudhayfah (Allah be pleased with him), the Prophet (peace and blessings of Allah be upon him) said: The tale-carrier will not enter Paradise.

All humans must stay away from the causes that lead to hatred and hostility between people, which divide them and break their unity.

The wise man does not immerse his thoughts in all this and does not accept the slanderer's backbiting or his tricks, because of his knowledge of the slanderer's punishment in the Hereafter.

Al-Kurayzi recited the following poem:

He who peddles between people, his scorpions are never safe from a friend and his vipers are never safe

Like one who travels by night

Where he comes from and where he is going, no one knows

Woe to the approval he gives, because he violates it

Woe to the love that comes from him, because it flies away.

The wise man must not take into account the words of the slanderer and must abstain from what is not appropriate to him while chasing away thoughts that betray intelligence.

He who gossips about a person says more about himself than about the person he is gossiping about.

Hammad ibn Salamah said: A man offered to sell his slave to another.

[The slave] said: "You will be safe from any tale-carrying from me."

So he decided to buy him based on that.

The slave visited his mistress and said to her: "Your husband does not love you.

He buys servants and marries them.

Do you want him to love and appreciate you?"

She replied: "Yes!"

He then said: "Take a razor and cut some hair from under his beard, then burn them for him like incense."

Then he went to the man and said, "Your wife is cheating on you and planning to murder you.

Do you want me to prove it to you?"

The man replied: "Yes!"

The slave said: "Then tonight, pretend to be asleep."

The man pretended to be asleep and when his wife approached him with the razor to cut hairs from his beard, he grabbed her and killed her. Later, his wife's family caught and killed him.

This example and others are the fruits of tale-carrying, because it tears the veil, reveals secrets, breeds resentment and malice, dissipates love, renews hostility, divides communities, awakens resentment and increases the aversion.

Thus, anyone who hears a defamatory statement about a brother must reprimand the author of these statements if they are true, accept his apologies and refrain from blaming him excessively.

He must also accustom himself to being grateful during good times, patient during bad times, and reprimanding when wronged (A person should not verify what the tale-carrier told him and should not believe in it and should not accept it).

'Ali ibn Muhammad al-Bassami recited the following verses:

I blame my brothers and stay with them

After their scolding, I don't cut it with them

And I forgive the one who makes mistakes

If he recognizes them and obeys willingly

The reprimand and blame of the tolerant pushes me to question myself,

I am not concerned about the ignorance of the ignorant.

Chapter 31: Accepting Excuses

According to Jawdan, the Messenger of Allah (peace and blessings of Allah be upon him) said: He who apologizes to his brother without him accepting it, then he has made the same mistake as a tax collector.

If someone apologizes for a past offense or mistake, the wise person should accept them and treat the person as if they had never done anything wrong.

Indeed, if we offer him an apology and he refuses it, then I fear that he will not join the Prophet (peace and blessings of Allah be upon him) at the Basin (the Hawd – the pool or lake in Jannah).

As for the one who errs in his behavior towards his brother, he must apologize to him.

Muhammad ibn'Abdillah ibn Zinji al-Baghdadi recited the following poem to me:

If one day a friend apologizes to you for a mistake

A brother's excuse should be accepted wholeheartedly

So spare him your harshness and forgive him

For indulgence is a quality in every man who has nobility in him.

The individual should not apologize to someone who does not want to accept them.

He should also not repeat his apologies to a brother several times, as this only leads to suspicion.

I actually prefer that excuses be kept to a minimum in any situation, because I know that excuses often turn into lies.

I have rarely seen someone apologize without mixing their excuses with lies.

The one who apologizes deserves to be forgiven, because apologizing for a mistake requires humility which itself involves calming angry feelings.

If the person is sincere in their apology, they will be humble in both their words and actions.

Apologies dispel sadness and hurt and block hostility and hatred.

A small number of excuses encompass a large number of mistakes and bad actions.

On the other hand, a lot of excuses lead to suspicion.

Even if there were no other benefit in apologizing other than that it lessens arrogance, it would be enough for the wise man to sincerely apologize every time he makes a mistake.

'Abd Al-Rahman ibn 'Anbasah ibn Sa'id visited Ma'n ibn Za'idah in Yemen when the two did not like each other.

When [Ma'n] saw him, he said: O 'Abd Al-Rahman, with what face did you come to me? And what good do you expect from me?

He replied: "May Allah rectify the leader.

Listen to me while I recite to you two verses from a poem that 'Abd Al-'Aziz ibn Marwan recited to me."

Ma'n said: "And what are they?"

'Abd Al-Rahman recited the following poem:

If there were a creature on this earth whose works

Were like yours, I would tell him "Stop!

But others seek to be excused

By those who seek reward.

Ma'n then said: "Certainly, I no longer hold it against you for the past and I would not reprimand you for the rest."

Chapter 32: The Secret

Narrated Abu Hurayrah (Allah be pleased with him), the Messenger of Allah (peace and blessings of Allah be upon him) said: Seek the protection of your goods (possessions) by keeping them secret, because for every benefit there is an envious person.

He who seeks to tread the path of the wise and intelligent must keep his thoughts secret.

He must not reveal what he is hiding from anyone, whether he considers the person trustworthy or not.

Indeed, it is possible that the relationship with another will change one day.

The latter will then reveal what he kept secret out of malice towards the other.

'Amr ibn al-'As (Allah be pleased with him) said: "I am amazed at a man who tries to escape fate, at a man who sees his brother's faults while ignoring his own and of a man who mentions his brother's bad sides while forgetting his own bad sides without ever feeling remorse for anything.

I never regretted anything, because I never revealed my secrets to anyone.

And how could I blame the one in whom I confided, when it was I who would have burdened him with the burden of my secret?"

'Abd Al-'Aziz ibn Salman recited the following verses to me:

A person's chest becomes tight due to secrets

So they were thrown into my chest and it tightened.

So who will blame me for revealing a secret when it was revealed to me first?

So the possessor of this secret is foolish.

He who keeps his secrets will find that it improves the way he manages his affairs.

Indeed, his faults will be hidden when he makes mistakes.

One with self-control and determination keeps their secrets locked in their heart.

The secret is a deposit.

Spreading it is treason.

The heart is the vault of secrets.

Some hearts tighten and become cluttered when a secret is placed there.

Others expand to encompass any secrets stored there.

Al-Kurayzi recited:

Make your heart a home for your secrets

Into which your tongue cannot enter.

If the tongue is capable of touching,

What the heart wants to hide,

You will see your secret in your friend

And everywhere else, even among your enemies.

Being too lax with secrets is a weakness.

He who hides something from his enemy does not necessarily have to reveal it to his friend.

Those gifted with understanding and observation are satisfied with what they have learned through experience.

They know who will keep a secret hidden and who will spread it, because the secret is only a secret if it is not revealed.

Chapter 33: The Consultation

According to Abu Mas'ud (Allah be pleased with him), the Prophet (peace and blessings of Allah be upon him) said: He who is consulted is entrusted.

He who holds a secret must keep it deep within himself, as previously mentioned.

On the other hand, if he feels that he must necessarily share it, he must do so by consulting the religious, intelligent and loved one.

He should never seek advice from anyone who does not possess these three characteristics.

If he is not religious, he will betray you.

If he is not intelligent, he will make a mistake about the best way to act.

If he is not liked, he may not give sincere advice.

Al-Zinji recited this poem to me:

O possessor of knowledge, ask about what you do not know

Questions are a cure for stammering and stuttering.

He whose evil you fear, do not consult him

Nor the foolish and careless.

Know that if you consult one of them,

You will have made him the head of a precious subject.

If you are looking for advice or are concerned about a matter,

So be suspicious and cautious of the one you prefer.

Look with your eyes at what can be seen,

And look with your heart at what has not appeared.

We confide in the person consulted, but their opinion is not a guarantee.

The person who consults protects himself from error and has the choice of accepting the opinion of the person consulted or refusing it.

The wise man who follows the path of those endowed with knowledge must know that consultation involves revealing one's secrets.

He must therefore never consult anyone other than the intelligent, the sincere, the beloved and the pious.

The guidance of advising is a blessing.

The consultation itself is a benefit when it is done with those described above.

If we ask people for advice, then the wise man must be the last to offer his advice, because he is the most apt to think intelligently, the furthest from mistakes, the closest to prudence and the safest in the face of error

.

Whoever seeks advice, let him make every effort to avoid taking it from the weak-minded, just as the determined person does not seek help from the lazy.

There is guidance in the consultation.

He who seeks advice does not lack intelligence, and he who does not seek advice is not safe from sin.

Those who consult a counselor do not regret it.

Al-Wasiti recited this poem to me:

The anxiety that prevents effort

Is a disease of the heart and body.

The reliability of the sensitive man

Appears when faced with grief.

If his sources of sustenance are inaccessible,

Then clear-sightedness is the best support

And if his plans have been derailed,

He seeks guidance by consulting his beloved brothers.

One of the traits of the wise man is that, when an answer escapes him, he consults the sincere, the wise who has good judgment, then follows him, recognizes the truth and does not persist in error.

Rather, he accepts the truth from anyone who brings it to him.

He does not look down on intelligent advice even when it comes from a base person, because the valuable pearl is not tainted by the lack of nobility of the fisherman who finds it.

So let him perform the prayer of seeking (Allah's) guidance (istikharah) and continue with what he was advised.

Chapter 34: Good Advice

According to Tamim al-Dari (Allah be pleased with him), the Prophet (peace and blessings of Allah be upon him) said: Certainly religion is good advice, certainly religion is good advice, certainly religion is good advice."

We asked: "To whom, O Messenger of Allah?"

The Prophet (peace and blessings of Allah be upon him) replied: "To Allah, to His Book, to His Messenger, to the leaders of the Muslims and to Muslims in general."

The wise man must maintain his sincerity and good advice towards Muslims.

He must renounce disloyalty towards them by not hiding his thoughts, words and actions.

Indeed, the Prophet (peace and blessings of Allah be upon him) ordered his Companions, when they pledged allegiance to him, to advise all Muslims in parallel with the performance of prayer and the payment of Zakah.

'Ali ibn Abi Talib (Allah be pleased with him) said: "Do not be disloyal, for this is a vile trait.

Show sincere affection for your brother by advising him, whether it is good or bad, and be with him wherever he goes."

Al-Kurayzi recited this poem to me:

Tell the good advisor who secretly offers us

The gift of his counsel, and places upon his shoulders a heavy obligation

That the council does not have precise limits that it must respect

Good advice is both strange and familiar

If the result is made apparent to us

This is a sermon from him and a warning

If the character of good advice were clear

We would not have known poverty

But the advice rather goes through different routes

Some work for some people, whether they know about it or not.

Humans have guidance of varying degrees

Advice is given, broken or rejected.

Good advice is obligatory for every Muslim, as mentioned earlier.

However, it must only be given in private, for whoever advises his brother in public will dishonor him, and whoever advises him in private will bring honor to him.

It is better for a Muslim to strive to beautify and honor his brother than to demean and embarrass him.

Sufyan said: I said to Mis'ar: Would you like someone to tell you about all your faults?

He replied: "As for him who comes to me to rebuke me through them, then no.

But if he comes advising me, then yes."

Ibn al-Mubarak said: "What used to be done was that when a man saw something he did not like in his brother, he would advise him privately.

He was then rewarded for his advice and for having done it in private.

Nowadays, if a man sees something he doesn't like, he angers his brother and destroys his privacy."

Ibn Zinji al-Baghdadi recited this poem to me:

How many announce their advice to you in public like enemies,

By low blows, deception is achieved

How many friends and advisors have you betrayed

By not following their guidance?

The judgment of each case, its final result depends

This is when secret and public information will appear.

Chapter 35: Do Not Boycott Muslims

Anas (Allah be pleased with him) reported that the Messenger of Allah (peace and blessings of Allah be upon him) said: Do not hate one another, do not be jealous of one another, do not turn your backs on one another, and do not be hostile to one another.

O servants of Allah, be brothers.

It is not permitted for a Muslim not to speak to his brother for more than three days.

Muslims are not permitted to hate, to be jealous, nor to turn their backs on each other.

It is obligatory for them to be brothers as Allah and His Messenger have ordered.

If one of them suffers, the others feel his pain.

If he is happy, others are happy for him.

Deception and evil are invalidated by submission to Allah by being satisfied with whatever Allah has legislated.

Muslims should not boycott each other because of a mistake.

Rather, they should treat each other with kindness, sympathy, compassion and not break up.

'Amr ibn Muhammad ibn 'Abdillah al-Nasawi recited the following poem to me.

Being boycotted by the nobles causes me great harm,

I consider turning away from my friend to be like death.

I can tolerate an old camel covered in sores,

In times of misfortune, but not of being abandoned.

Three things lead to the boycott of one Muslim by another:

· - Due to a mistake made by his brother, and everyone makes mistakes: he doesn't turn a blind eye to it and doesn't look for other good characteristics.

· - Due to a lie from a slanderer who changes his feelings towards his brother. He does not question this lie or make excuses for it.

· - Due to the weariness of one towards the other, because boredom can lead to the breakdown of the relationship and there is no friend for the boring person.

Ibn Shubramah had a brother who broke up with him.

He then wrote him the following poem:

Neither of us needs our brother here on earth,

But if we die, we will need each other even less in the afterlife.

It is not permitted for a Muslim to boycott his brother for more than three days.

Whoever does this will have committed what the Prophet (peace and blessings of Allah be upon him) prohibited.

The better of the two is the one who greets the other first with "Al-Salam 'Alaykum".

The first to give salam will be the first to enter Paradise.

He who breaks with his brother for a whole year, it is as if he had shed his blood.

Whoever dies after breaking up with his brother will enter Hell unless Allah forgives him and shows him mercy.

The limit within which a Muslim is allowed to boycott his brother is three days.

Chapter 36: Tolerance

According to Abu Sa'id al-Khudri (Allah be pleased with him), the Prophet (peace and blessings of Allah be upon him) said: Only he who has experienced failure can be tolerant (forgiving), and only those with experience can be wise.

This hadith is an example of what is mentioned in the book Fusul al-Sunan: the Arabs relate a word to a thing because it is close to being complete and deny a word from a thing due to the absence of a complete character.

Thus, the Prophet (peace and blessings of Allah be upon him) negated the word "tolerant" for one who has never experienced failure or disappointment, due to lack of completeness, for it is rare that one who has never been disappointment is forgiving.

The lenient is characterized by an elevated nature, high stature, commendable temperament and decent deeds.

Indulgence (tolerance) is a word used to describe the ability to refrain from doing something forbidden when exposed to something one hates.

Tolerance implies knowledge, patience, perseverance and then determination.

There is nothing better than combining forgiveness with the ability (to take revenge).

Indulgence is the best form of revenge.

Muhammad ibn 'Abdillah ibn Zinji al-Baghdadi recited this poem to me:

Do you not see that indulgence (tolerance) makes you stronger and more beautiful

for the one who possesses it, and ignorance is a dishonor to him who chooses it

So bury evil with good and composure

Because good buries evil and fear.

Among the examples that illustrate the importance of the word indulgence as well as its high status is the fact that Allah the Noble, the Most High, named Himself with this word, and then only described Abraham and Ishmael in the Quran by the quality of indulgence when He said: Surely Abraham was compassionate and tolerant. So we gave him the good news of a patient boy (Ishmael).

If indulgence had no other qualities than that of preventing the individual from committing sins and falling into error, then it would have been obligatory for the wise to be tolerant (forgiving) and patient whenever he finds a reason to be.

Indulgence comes either from the natural character of the person or from acquisition following its practice, or from these two sources.

Abu al-Darda (Allah be pleased with him) said: "Knowledge is attained only through learning, and indulgence is attained only through patience."

He who aspires to good does good, and he who seeks protection from evil is protected.

Al-Kurayzi recited this poem to me:

If, with a similar action, I respond to ignorance

So I'm no different from the ignorant if I debate with him

But I am approached by the thoughtless,

Then I will overcome him through indulgence.

The wise man is patient and forgiving with people.

If it becomes difficult, let him pretend to be patient, for this will elevate him to the level of indulgence.

Forbearance begins with understanding, then resolution, then determination, then restraint, then patience, then contentment, then silence and endurance.

What is better than responding to aggression with good? As for doing good to one who does good to you or being lenient to one who does you no harm, that is neither benevolence nor indulgence.

Indulgence is of two types:

· - the first is that Allah tests his servant with a test and that the wise man is patient and restrains himself through endurance from doing something that is not appropriate for him.

· - the second is being exposed to what we hate from the creation. So whoever makes indulgence (tolerance) a habit, it is not necessary for him to force himself to be patient.

Chapter 37: Moderation

Narrated Abu al-Darda (Allah be pleased with him), the Messenger of Allah (peace and blessings of Allah be upon him) said: He who has received a portion of moderation has received a portion of good, and he who has been deprived of his portion of moderation has been deprived of his portion of good.

The wise must be gentle and moderate in all circumstances and not hasty and impetuous, because Allah loves moderation in everything.

He who is deprived of moderation is deprived of good.

Goals of a person can hardly be achieved without balancing forbearance (moderation) and hastiness.

The individual can hardly achieve his goal without a balance between moderation and eagerness.

Mansur ibn Muhammad al-Kurayzi said in the following poem:

Moderation is the most reliable thing you can follow

Ignorance is the most sinister thing a man can follow

Goes from praise to success the one endowed with determination

He who has moderation does not accumulate errors.

The wise man must be moderate at all times and balanced in all situations.

Indeed, desiring something excessively is bad, just as being lax in what is required constitutes weakness.

What cannot be resolved by moderation and gentleness cannot be resolved by harshness.

There is no better guide than moderation and nothing more reliable than wisdom.

From moderation comes prudence, and from prudence comes reliability.

However, lack of moderation leads to clumsiness, and from clumsiness comes the fear of error.

Al-Abrash recited the following verses to me:

You must face moderation and walk its path,

In injustice there is destruction and in moderation there is a way

If you don't recognize its importance to you,

Support its weight, because if you can't you will be ruined.

Moderation is rarely taken by surprise just as eagerness is rarely taken by surprise.

Likewise, calm rarely knows regret and he who speaks too much is rarely spared from error.

The hasty person speaks before knowing, responds before being questioned, praises something before trying it, denigrates before complimenting, shows determination before studying the situation, and acts before being determined.

Haste is accompanied by regret and detached from peace.

The Arabs used to call haste: "the mother of regret".

Some people of knowledge recited this poem to me:

Weakness is a disadvantage and prudence contains nothing that is not good

The highest degree of caution is to not trust people.

Do not neglect caution in situations of distrust,

If you are safe then what is the downside of being careful?

Hastiness comes from recklessness.

You will see that the hasty person is still not complimented even when his impetuosity pays off.

On the other hand, he is blamed when it fails.

The hasty person does not move forward without deviating from his goal and what is important, urgently seeking something rougher, more difficult, a more complicated path to find.

He makes decisions like a fool.

Haste is the representative of regret.

No one acts hastily without earning regret and ridicule, because mistakes come from haste.

Taking an action after reflection is safer than stopping after rushing to act.

The hasty is never subject to praise, but the wise knows that not to act is a weakness.

He then avoids these two extremes and makes his path a middle path.

Chapter 38: Eloquence

According to Ibn 'Umar (Allah be pleased with him), the Messenger of Allah (peace and blessings of Allah be upon him) said: Certainly, eloquence is a form of magic.

He (peace be upon him) compared eloquence to magic in this hadith, because the magician leads the hearts of those who behold his magic to be bewitched by him.

In the same way, one who expresses himself eloquently can lead people to be amazed and captivated by the poetry of his words.

It is then that their souls long to be close to him and their eyes long to look upon him.

Al-Kurayzi recited this poem to me:

Honor the person of good behavior, honor the person of noble heritage

Indeed, determination is only found among those endowed with good manners and a good heritage.

There are two kinds of people: those with intelligence and those with good behavior

Like gold and white silver

All the rest of humanity is not good

They are only Arabs or supporters.

Eloquence is the best adornment a man can wear.

Good manners are a companion in times of loneliness, friendliness in poverty, status in congregations, an increase in wisdom, and a sign of good behavior.

He who learns good manners in his youth will benefit from them in adulthood.

In fact, the palm tree is more likely to produce fruit if it is pollinated when young.

He who speaks eloquently is not regarded in the same way by people of knowledge and wisdom than he who expresses himself incorrectly.

Muhammad ibn 'Abdillah al-Baghdadi recited this poem to me:

O he who seeks glory through his lineage

A mother and a father each owned

Do you think they are made of money

Or copper, gold or steel?

Where do you think they are superior in their creation

That they are more than flesh and bones and veins?

Rather, superiority comes from gentleness

Good manners and good behavior.

The best thing a father can leave behind for his son is a good compliment and good manners.

However, in my opinion, the silent one is better than the one who speaks eloquently but lies, just as the one who does not desire women is better than the fornicator.

Therefore, the wise man must illuminate his heart with good manners, in the same way as fire is lit by wood.

Indeed, whoever does not illuminate his heart will sink into darkness.

Anyone who learns good manners should not do so in order to use them as a training tool for a competition.

Rather, his intention must be to benefit his person and use them to please his Creator.

The words are like luminous pearls, green emeralds, and red rubies.

On the other hand, some are better than others, because some words are like clay, rock, dust and mud.

Those who learn good manners and eloquence the most are the scholars because of the time they spend reading ahadith and the depth to which it delves into the different branches of knowledge.

Chapter 39: Lawful Gain of Wealth

According to 'Amr ibn al-'As (Allah be pleased with him), the Messenger of Allah (peace and blessings of Allah be upon him): O 'Amr, the virtuous money possessed by the virtuous person is a blessing.

This hadith clearly shows that the Prophet (peace and blessings of Allah be upon him) allowed the accumulation of goods for those who fulfill their obligations.

This can be seen in his description of both money and the owner of that money in terms of virtue.

It also shows that amassing wealth is permissible only if it is not prohibited and for one who amasses and spends it in a way that fulfills his obligations to Allah.

Mansur ibn Muhammad al-Kurayzi recited the following poem:

If what you have gathered is not good,

So you are the furthest from people,

Because this is the result of your bad deeds.

You are the one who makes it an object of reward or destruction.

Indeed, the most important things that an individual can benefit from in this life and after death are piety and good works.

Thus, during his youth, the sage must strive to correct his errors and improve his level of worship.

His money must be used to improve his life, protect his person, prepare for his afterlife and satisfy his Creator.

On the other hand, know that poverty is better than wealth obtained through illicit means.

A rich man without principles is more despicable than a dog, even if he is productive and efficient.

The happiest people are those who, when they are rich, are humble, and when poor are content, because no one has found a way out of poverty by being arrogant.

Poverty can cause a decline in intelligence and honor, knowledge and good manners.

It can even lead to disbelief.

Someone who is known for his poverty can attract suspicion and accusations.

He is often tested by difficulties and trials.

However, by Allah, this is not the case of the one whom Allah has blessed with a pure and humble heart, who sees the reward prepared for him due to his pain endured in this life.

Therefore, he is not concerned about the difficulties of this life nor those that creatures inflict on him.

Poverty leads to degradation and wealth leads to respect.

As he saw correctly who said:

A person's wealth can hide their mistakes

We believe everything he says, even if he's a liar

The intelligence of the poor is ridiculed

People think he is stupid, even though his intelligence is high.

Every characteristic that is praised when exhibited by the rich is considered a vice when exhibited by the poor.

So, if a poor person is patient and forgiving, we say he is stupid.

If he is wise, we say he is clever.

If he is eloquent, they say he is talking nonsense.

If he is intelligent, they say he is tough.

If he is silent, they say he is stupid.

If he is cautious, we say he is cowardly.

If he is determined, he is said to be reckless.

If he is generous, he is said to be a waster.

If he is thrifty, we say he is miserly.

The worst form of wealth is that acquired from illicit sources and spent on things that benefit no one.

Money is never acquired, even if it is invested and reinvested.

Rather, it is a part and a gift from the All-Knowing Creator.

Al-Abrash recited the following poem to me:

Some men are unhappy and others are unhappy in their company

And Allah makes people happy through others

The sustenance of man in his youth does not come from cunning.

Happiness in livelihood and wealth

Is like a hunter who misses his prey even though he is experienced,

While one who is not a hunter can be blessed by catching it.

The worst form of wealth is that which the owner does not use to fulfill his obligations.

Worse than this is money obtained from illicit sources, which is not used for obligations and is spent on forbidden things.

Investing money and using it in moderation allows you to have a healthy life.

Man must purify his possessions, for no one is above this need, whether pious or evil.

The wise should not expect the blessings of Allah to last forever, so much so that he delays fulfilling his obligations with that money (like Hajj), because he who is not grateful for benefit will see this benefit taken away from him and given to another.

Chapter 40: Honor (manliness, chivalry, etc)

According to Abu Hurayrah (Allah be pleased with him), the Prophet (peace and blessings of Allah be upon him) said: A man's nobility depends on his religion, his honor, his intelligence, his lineage, and his behavior.

The wise person must maintain a sense of honor by which he possesses good character and eliminates his faults.

Some rely on the reputation and nobility of their father and grandfather without carrying themselves with the same level of character and good works that they achieved.

Mansur ibn Muhammad recited to me a poem that blames this kind of person:

Some do not achieve honor

They inherit a father then lose theirs

His soul invites him to behave obscenity

It prevents him from seeking the highest degrees

He obeys him then is afflicted by a calamity

While the honorable person bases his honor on these degrees.

I have never seen anyone make a worse deal, suffer worse afflictions, fail more, or be more misguided than one who assimilates himself to his ancestors and their prodigious behavior while abandoning their way and example.

This kind of person presumptuously wants their status to be high and to hold a position of authority over others because of their ancestry.

What nonsense ! Indeed, a man only obtains position and respect, in reality, through his own actions.

He can only become noble in this life and the hereafter through hard work.

Al-Bassami recited this poem to me:

How many times have you heard someone say "I am the son of such and such a tribe?"

Now this tribe was destroyed and its reputation lost

His two pillars have fallen and he laments having been supported

It ruins its ending and rectifies its beginning.

People differ about "honor", but in my opinion it consists of two characteristics:

- avoid actions that Allah and Muslims hate

- display behavior that Allah and Muslims like.

The wise man must improve himself by his honor as much as he is able and this is difficult without money.

So he who has received goods, but is too miserly to invest them in his own honor, has lost this life and the next.

Furthermore, he is not safe from being surprised by death, separated from his possessions and placed in his grave alone.

Then, once he leaves, his goods are inherited by people who consume them without praising him or thanking him.

How regrettable that is! What pain can be greater than this?

The wise man must avoid that which leads people to despise him, because it tarnishes his honor.

Indeed, despicable acts are the opposite of honor and lead to an individual's reputation being damaged.

They bring him to degradation and humiliation.

Chapter 41: Generosity

According to Abu Hurayrah (Allah be pleased with him), the Prophet (peace and blessings of Allah be upon him) said: The generous one is close to Allah and close to people.

The miser is far from Allah and far from people.

The generous ignorant person is more loved by Allah than the miserly devotee.

Allah can grant you all the wealth of this ephemeral world then take it all back and give it to another without it benefiting you for the future life unless you have prepared good works.

It is then essential for the wise to strive to use their money to fulfill their financial obligations, thereby aiming for reward in the afterlife and a positive memory in this world.

Generosity is loved and praised, while greed is hated and criticized.

There is no good in money that is not accompanied by generosity, just as there is no good in words that have no meaning.

Al-Muntasr ibn Bilal recited this poem to me:

Greed is a deficiency and generosity is an honorable trait

With Allah, greed and generosity are not equal

In poverty there is character and in ease there is peace

When it comes to wealth, people are either blessed or limited.

The most generous are those who are generous with their money and careful with the money of others.

When people are generous, they are elevated in ranks.

When they are greedy, they are belittled.

Generosity protects honor just as forgiveness purifies intelligence and wisdom.

Complete generosity consists of giving without expecting anything in return and without having people indebted to you, because he who gives without expecting anything in return is blessed with abundance.

Reminding people of your generosity destroys your good works.

Whether you can remove from your generous actions a cover with two edges: one side which consists of reminding people of your generosity and another which consists of expecting a reward for it, then this is the greatest form of generosity.

In reality, this is true generosity.

Among the best qualities a person can possess is generosity done without reminding people of your favors towards them and without expecting anything in return.

There is also indulgence and patience without weakness or humiliation.

The basis of generosity is to refrain from withholding people's rights, just as the basis of a healthy body is to restrain from eating, drinking, and sexual intercourse.

So, just as honor and nobility are of no use without humility, and saving is of no use until one has what one needs, so life has no use without goods (wealth) and goods are of no use without generosity.

Just as affinities come from love, praise comes from giving.

Al-Kurayzi recited this poem to me:

Greed reveals a person's flaws to people,

And generosity hides them.

Cover yourself with the garment of generosity,

Because I think it can hide all the flaws from people's eyes.

The person who is least generous (that is tight) with his money is called a cheapskate.

He who is arrogant and extreme in his stinginess is said to be stingy.

As for the one who praises the stingy person and makes excuses for his actions, he is called a miser.

There is no characteristic that more tarnishes a person's honor and is more harmful to his faith than greed.

I have never seen a person, from the East to the West, who possessed the values of generosity and indulgence without him being someone who faced his own problems and overcame obstacles .

People who knew him and those who didn't knew him behaved with humility towards him.

So, if you want to enjoy a high status in the afterlife and in this life, be generous with your wealth and refrain from harming others.

On the other hand, whoever wants to tarnish his honor, harm his faith, exhaust his friends and alienate his neighbors, let him continue to be stingy and miserly.

Chapter 42: Accepting Gifts

Narrated 'Abdullah ibn Mas'ud (Allah be pleased with him), the Messenger of Allah (peace and blessings of Allah be upon him) said: Accept invitations.

Don't reject gifts.

Don't hit Muslims.

The Prophet (peace and blessings of Allah be upon him) warned in this hadith not to refuse gifts that come from Muslims.

So, whoever receives a gift must accept it.

Then, he will be rewarded if he is grateful.

Indeed, I like Muslims to give gifts to each other, because the act of giving gives rise to love and the disappearance of resentment.

When Abu Hanifah stood up and left an assembly, Masawir al-Waraq said to the people:

Before that day we were comfortable in matters of religion,

Until we are tested by the people of analogy

A people who, when they come together, shout by example

Foxes sniffing between the coffins.

When this came to the ears of Abu Hanifah, he sent a gift to Masawir who then said:

And as for those who judge us by analogy

By memorable and strange fatawas

They came up with correct analogies

Correct because of the example of Abu Hanifah.

If the jurist listens to him, he is attentive,

And affirms it with ink on paper.

Therefore, the wise man should offer gifts to his peers as much as he can, with the aim of winning their affection and avoiding their hostility.

Al-Abrash recited this poem to me:

People who give each other gifts

End up uniting their hearts

The gift sows love and friendship in the heart

Establishes reverence and dignity

He catches hearts without chasing them

It grants love and beauty.

The wise man must use what is available to him at any given time to achieve the desired results.

He should not hope for what he does not have, even if he has little.

Al-Mughirah ibn Shu'bah (Allah be pleased with him) was asked: What still makes you happy?"

He replied: "Doing good works for my brothers. "

He was asked: "Who are those who have the best livelihood?"

He replied: "Those who support each other in their sustenance."

He was also asked: "Who are those who have the worst livelihood?"

He replied: "Those who do not support each other in their sustenance."

Chapter 43: Help

Narrated Abu Hurayrah (Allah be pleased with him), the Messenger of Allah (peace and blessings of Allah be upon him) said: Whoever relieves a believer of a worry among the worries of this world, Allah relieves him of a worry among the worries of the Day of Judgment.

Whoever grants ease to his debtor, Allah eases him in this world and in the Hereafter.

Whoever covers a believer, Allah covers him in this world and in the Hereafter.

Allah helps the servant as long as the servant helps his brother.

It is obligatory for all Muslims to advise other Muslims and help them dispel their sadness and difficulty.

Indeed, whoever relieves someone in this life will have their burdens relieved on the Day of Judgment.

He who exerts effort to fulfill the need of another, but is unable to do so, will be rewarded as if he had spared no pain or expense for it.

Even the smallest effort deserves praise.

The true colors of your friends appear in times of difficulty, just like family when they are tested in times of poverty.

Indeed, in times of ease and comfort (wealth), everyone is a friend.

The worst people are those who abandon their brothers in times of difficulty and need, just as the worst countries are those that have no fertile soil or security.

Al-Kurayzi recited this poem to me:

A young man's best days are his most useful days

Design a culture and production that lasts the longest

You do not achieve good through evil works

The farmer only reaps what he sows

Every day is different

Some days the young man will experience lows and some days he will experience highs.

He who knows the reward of helping others will spare no effort to help in any way, even before he is asked, so that he may reap as many rewards as possible and so that he avoid regretting any missed opportunity to help.

The wise man knows that he who possesses a blessing is not immune from losing it.

He knows that the best works are done before he is asked to do them.

Abu al-'Atahiyah met Al-Rashid who said:

« O Abu al-'Atahiyah, ask from me anything."

He replied: "If success is achieved by sacrificing honor, then I am far from achieving it."

One should not beg when asking for something, even in times of need.

Indeed, sometimes asking insistently can lead the person to refuse to help.

The search for well-being is like a game of chance: sometimes you win and sometimes you lose.

So if you get what you need, you should praise Allah.

If you are refused the help you ask for, then you must be satisfied with this situation.

You should only ask for help in private and not in public places, assemblies, or mosques.

'Umar ibn al-Khattab said: "Do not ask people in assemblies and mosques, exposing them for all to see.

Instead, ask them at home, so that he who gives may give, and he who refuses may refuse."

'Umar ibn Al-Khattab, may Allah be pleased with him, said that if the person one asks is generous, but unable to help, then asking him in front of others will cause him embarrassment and shame.

On the other hand, if the person being asked is stingy, then asking them in front of others in a congregation or a mosque will probably urge him to give to the person in need, because one who is miserly will not give out of piety or honor, but to be mentioned and complimented by people.

As for me, I prefer that the wise be patient in times of need.

If possible, let him refrain from asking the miser for anything.

Indeed, if he gives it will be dishonor and if he refuses it will be death.

Chapter 44: Responding Favorably to Requests

Jabir (Allah be pleased with him) reports: I have never asked the Prophet (peace and blessings of Allah be upon him) for something and he said no.

And he never hit anything with his hand.

I like a man to make an effort to excel in his behavior and to refrain from refusing to respond favorably to someone's request for help or money.

Indeed, lacking money is better than lacking good behavior and regretting having missed the opportunity to help someone.

The truly free man is the one who is liberated by his good manners, just like the worst slave is the one chained by his bad behavior.

Al-Baghdadi recited this poem to me:

Control your desires if virtue is important to you

Fearing that obstacles will appear and end up defeating you

If you are concerned about evil, then take it into account

By avoiding situations that should be avoided.

The more a person gives of his possessions, the more noble he becomes.

If it were not for the generosity of righteous people, many poor people would have died.

We do not deserve the titles of "noble" and "generous" by simply preventing evil, without this being coupled with beneficence towards others.

The one who loves to do good and for whom helping others is important, people will flock to him full of hope.

He who lives for himself and does not help anyone else with his livelihood will experience a short life in terms of good works, even if he lives to a ripe old age.

The unhappy and the miserable are those who live a long time without helping others or doing good works.

He who does not help others is weak.

Anyone who finds fault in others, but makes excuses for himself for the same mistakes, is an imposter who needs counseling.

He who has no ambition and no principles other than his stomach and his private parts is no better than an animal.

Ambition is very important as is maintaining a rank, because people are judged by their ambitions.

The wise man must begin with good works and generosity towards those who deserve it most.

He must therefore start with his family, then his brothers, then his neighbors and so on.

Study how the pious and the learned give alms and do good works; some of them completely refrain from acting in a manner contrary to the order we have cited.

The wise man should give before he is asked, because meeting someone's needs before he asks is better than fulfilling his request and refraining from refusing the request of the needy is better than to humiliate him.

The good deed is beautified by its accomplishment and by taking care of it after having accomplished it, because by rectifying its end, you purify its beginning.

Giving after refusing is better than refusing after giving.

People are of two kinds when it comes to good works done to others: grateful and ungrateful.

Chapter 45: Hospitality

Narrated Abu Hurayrah (Allah be pleased with him), the Messenger of Allah (peace and blessings of Allah be upon him) said: He who believes in Allah and the Last Day should honor his guest, and he who believes in Allah and the Last Day should not harm his neighbor.

I prefer that the wise man feed people and often entertain his guests, because feeding people is one of the noblest forms of generosity and one of the best qualities of people of knowledge and piety.

Those who are known for inviting people gain a reputation for nobility and dignity among those who know them and those who do not.

Honoring the guest elevates a person's status beyond imagination, even when he comes from a humble background.

He is blessed with sweet praise and abundance.

Those who achieved a position of authority before Islam and after Islam, who were famous for their status, who gained the loyalty of their people and to whom people traveled far and near, achieved it by nurturing people and honoring the guests.

The Arabs considered the pinnacle of generosity to be feeding others and honoring guests.

They didn't consider a person to be generous until they had walked a mile or two looking for a guest.

The wise man should often invite people and feed the poor, because the blessings of Allah are guarded and maintained by using them for good.

Otherwise, they will return where they came from.

Regret and the desire to get them back will not bring them back.

However, whoever fulfills the rights of Allah and the duties incumbent upon him in relation to his blessings will see them increase and his works will accumulate and will be kept for him for the Day of Judgment.

Among the important elements of hospitality is being grateful for what you have in the way of food, even if it is a small amount, and you present this to your guest, because he who is not grateful for what he has will not want to share it with his guests.

One of the ways to honor your guest is to have a good conversation with him, to welcome him with a smiling face, to serve him yourself, because there is no shame in serving your guest, just like there is no honor in making him serve you or asking for compensation for feeding him.

Muhammad ibn Suhayl recited this poem to me:

Certainly I smile at those who want to be entertained as a guest,

And my house is spacious to entertain my guests

From the moment he removes his saddle, I make my guest laugh

There is then abundance even in a place affected by aridity

There's not much for the guest to eat

But the generous face contains prosperity.

Chapter 46: Appreciation

Narrated Abu Hurayrah (Allah be pleased with him), the Messenger of Allah (peace and blessings of Allah be upon him) said: He who does not thank people has not thanked Allah.

The one who received a gift or kindness should show gratitude and return the same or better than what he received.

Indeed, giving back is not equivalent to having been the first to give, even if the gift is modest.

Those who are unable to give a gift in return should praise the person, because this can serve as recognition for a good deed and no one can do without praise and recognition.

Muhammad ibn Zinji al-Baghdadi recited this poem to me:

If the nobleman didn't need thanks

Because of his power and high rank

Allah would not have ordered his servants to show gratitude to Him

"O Men and Jinns, thank Me," he therefore said.

Sa'id ibn al-'As passed by a man's house in Madinah.

The man asked him for water, so he gave it to him.

Then he passed by a house up for auction.

He then asked the auctioneer: "Why are you selling this house?"

He replied: "The owner is in debt."

Sa'id ibn al-'As said: "Can I meet the owner?"

He then entered the house and found the owner sitting with his creditor.

He said to the owner: "Why are you selling your house?"

He replied: "I owe this man 4,000 dinars."

Sa'id ibn al-'As sat with the two men and chatted with them for a while.

Then he sent his servant somewhere and he returned with 10,000 dinars.

He gave 4000 to the creditor and the rest to the debtor.

Then, Sa'id ibn al-'As mounted his horse and continued on his way.

Al-Muntasr ibn Bilal recited this poem to me:

He who does you good, show yourself grateful to him,

Useful will then be his good deed

Do not be stingy in gratitude and repay the loan

Be the best receiver and giver of good.

The noble does not deny a benefit and does not become displeased in the face of a difficulty.

When he receives a benefit, he is grateful.

When he is tested by a difficulty, he is patient.

He who is ungrateful for small things will certainly be ungrateful for great blessings.

Benefits do not increase and do not protect against trials without the person being grateful to Allah and to the one who has done good deed towards him.

The wise man should be grateful for the blessings he receives and praise the good deed as much as he is able, as best he can.

Therefore, if he is able, he will do double the favor done to him, otherwise, he will act equivalently.

If he is unable to accomplish any of these things, he should show gratitude by making efforts to return the favor with gratitude and saying, "Jazak Allahu khayr" (may Allah reward you with good).

Some do not recognize the benefits.

These people fall into two categories:

· 1- One who does not understand the causes of blessings and the reasons to show gratitude, due to a lack of understanding or experience with loved ones and friends.

· If this is the case, you should turn a blind eye to him and not argue with him because of his lack of recognition and gratitude.

· 2- One who is intelligent, but who refuses to show recognition because of his contempt for others or to belittle the gift or the giver.

If this is the case, the wise person must abandon this type of behavior and never return to it.

If this is something he has developed a reputation for, then he needs to come out and make his regret known for acting in such a manner.

Chapter 47: Responsibility

According to Ibn 'Umar (Allah be pleased with him), the Messenger of Allah (peace and blessings of Allah be upon him) said: Each of you is a shepherd, and each of you will be questioned concerning his flock.

The ruler is a shepherd, the man is a shepherd to the people of his house, the woman is a shepherdess to her husband's house and to her children.

So every one of you is a shepherd, and every one of you will be questioned concerning his flock.

The Sunnah, as the chosen one taught us, clearly shows that everyone has responsibilities and that everyone must assume them.

It is therefore obligatory on anyone who holds responsibilities towards someone else to remain honest in their promise to them.

The shepherds of humanity are the scholars.

The shepherds of kings are their reasons.

The shepherds of the righteous are their pieties.

The shepherds of the students are their teachers.

The boys' shepherds are their fathers.

A woman's protector is her husband.

A slave's protector is his master.

Every shepherd is responsible for his flock.

It is of utmost importance that the ruler respects his pact to govern his people.

Leaders are among the most important types of shepherds who guide their flock, as their orders are usually followed.

Thus, the condition of people is improved or worsened depending on the choices of the leader.

So if the ruler does not use his time wisely and is not careful, he will be destroyed and will destroy his people.

A single corrupt leader can bring destruction to the entire world.

A leader's rule depends on the obedience of his followers.

This obedience depends on a good minister and counselor, pious and intelligent.

The salary of these important workers cannot be paid without money.

There can be no money without a prosperous society.

A society cannot prosper without justice.

Therefore, the position of the leader depends on the establishment of justice and of security.

Without these elements, his position will be precarious.

Thus, the leader must give the greatest importance to supervising the actions of his employees to the point that no action, bad or good, escapes his attention.

If the leader does not know what his employees are doing, he will not be able to achieve justice.

Any governance that is not based on fear and obedience to Allah is in reality a dictatorship and not governance.

Any leader who does not include obedience to Allah in his governance is like a caretaker of a garbage dump.

As some poets have said:

The governance of men without religion

And without piety is done unworthily

All governance without piety

Is more humiliating than sitting on trash

The noblest of homes, the highest strength

And the best governance consists of refraining from leading.

Al-Zuhri left the company of Hisham ibn 'Abd al-Malik and said: I have never witnessed a day like this and I have never heard remarks such as those made towards Hisham ibn 'Abd al-Malik a few moments ago.

A man said to him: O Commander of the Faithful, memorize these four sentences that I am about to tell you.

They will preserve your kingdom and rectify your people:

Do not think that something in which you do not believe can be completed.

Do not be seduced by the road to the summit, even if it was easy, because the decline will be steep and difficult.

Remember that those who are in your charge will get their reward.

So be careful of the consequences of your actions.

Those who are close to the leader should not hold back from advising him.

Indeed, if you do not advise him, let the doctors not inform him of an illness, let the brothers not tell him bad news, then you will only have betrayed yourself and let yourself down.

The ruler's companions are not immune from harm, just as he who rides a wild beast is not immune from dust.

Those who are close to the ruler should not think themselves safe from his anger when they tell him the truth, or safe from his punishment when they tell him a lie.

On the other hand, do not be presumptuous and disrespectful, because the intelligent does not drink poison just because he has the antidote.

I would like anyone who is tested by having to work with a leader to teach him the importance of fearing and obeying Allah, and doing good deeds, in a way that seems let him be the one to learn from the leader and teach him good behavior as if he were the one guided by the leader.

In this way, he will protect himself from the anger of the governor.

If this anger has a motive, then it is possible to calm it down, but if there is no reason behind it, then there is no hope.

There is no need for citizens to know everything the governor does regarding society, as this will only lead to chaos and instability.

How presumptuous it is to think that you can associate with governors without being tested by adversity! Who can follow their desires without suffering harm?

Sometimes a beautiful tree can be destroyed by its own succulent fruit.

The peacock can be killed because of its magnificent feathers, because due to the weight of its tail it is unable to escape from its predator.

Anyone who works with the governor will not be immune to his changing moods.

Rivers contain fresh water, but when they reach the sea they become salty.

Likewise, the scholar who stays away from the gates of kings increases the light of his knowledge.

On the other hand, the scholar who frequents kings covers his heart and prevents himself from acquiring more knowledge.

The companions of kings are not immune to their changing moods.

Those who stay away from them are not safe from their investigations.

It is obligatory for those who are responsible for the affairs of Muslims to return to Allah, the Noble and Most High, at every time and every opportunity, so that it is not corrupted by power.

In reality, the ruler must keep in mind the greatness of Allah, His Power, His Sovereignty and the fact that He is the One who will punish those who oppress others and reward those who do good.

In this way, the governor will behave in a way that will earn him rewards in this life and the next.

He must also ponder on the lives of those who were like him and who came before him.

Indeed, there is no doubt that he must be grateful for his situation and that he is responsible for his own account.

Chapter 48: Self-discipline

According to Abu al-Darda (Allah be pleased with him), the Prophet (peace and blessings of Allah be upon him) said: He who wakes up in the morning in good health, safe with his family and with the food of his day, it is as if all the riches of this world had been gathered for him.

The wise man must not allow himself to be seduced by life here below, its brilliance, its beauty, its magnificence.

He must not let himself be distracted by it and forget the afterlife and its eternal benefits.

Rather, he should give it little importance just as Allah gives it little importance, because this world will inevitably disappear.

Its cities will fall into ruin, its peoples will die, its magnificence will crumble, and its civilizations will disappear.

No one will escape death, from the arrogant governor to the poor sufferer.

Everyone will be reduced to dust and then tested until the moment of their resurrection.

The Knower of the Invisible will inherit the earth and everything it contains.

The wise man does not rely on such an abode.

He cannot find rest in a world endowed with such a description, especially when he knows what awaits him in the next life: what no eye has ever seen, what no ear has ever heard, what no heart can imagine.

He therefore abstains from this modest quantity and instead aspires to abundant benefit.

Al-Kurayzi recited this poem to me:

Time is just a succession of days and nights

Life is all about falling asleep and waking up

The human dies and the human lives

Time decides who will be blamed.

Life here below is a stormy sea.

Humans float in the depths of its waves waiting to drown.

This metaphor concerns all creatures and how appropriate it is! In fact, it simply describes the way in which everything is heading towards its end.

He who has three things in his life has everything this world has to offer: security, food, and good health.

Only swindlers and fraudsters are seduced by the things of this world.

Only the miser needs it.

The wise man knows that eternity cannot be exchanged for what is temporary.

So, for him, focusing on the things of this world that will be profitable in the afterlife makes more sense than gathering everything he can from this world without preparing anything as good works for his future life.

There is nothing more important and meaningful than your life and there is no greater failure than wasting it for anything other than eternal life.

He who wishes to be free must stay away from desires, even if they are pleasant.

He must know that not everything that is pleasant is necessarily beneficial, but everything that is beneficial is pleasant.

All desires are base except those that bring return or benefit.

There is no better return than Paradise, than being satisfied with Allah and not needing people.

'Ali ibn Muhammad al-Bassami recited this poem to me:

Give importance to patience at the right time

Because bad situations don't last forever

The universe revolves around us with its wonders

If he continues, he is like a sleeping dream

Happiness and sadness, recovery and remission

Until the time of destruction draws near

So, rely on Allah and seek his help instead of that of people

When one of the serious matters descends on you.

The wise man must relegate this lower world to its due place, refrain from relying on it and from needing it, while preparing what he can for his eternal life.

He achieves this by refraining from long hope and by constantly remembering death.

Distant hope is like a knife on the back of human necks.

The wise man must therefore move away from it, while meditating on the nations and generations that have gone before, on how every trace of their existence has been eliminated, to the point that everything that remains of them is a memory and all that remains of these cities are sketches.

Glory then to Him who is able to resurrect them for final retribution.

Chapter 49: Keeping Death in Mind

Narrated Abu Hurayrah (Allah be pleased with him), the Messenger of Allah (peace and blessings of Allah be upon him) said: Remember often the one who kills pleasures.

The wise man must remember death and refrain from being seduced by the life here below because of what we have mentioned previously in our book about the different branches of wisdom and reason.

Death is a cup that passes from person to person.

Every soul must inevitably drink from it and taste its taste.

Death is the one that kills all pleasures and ruins desires.

The wise man does not forget something he expects.

Something he knows could appear at any time.

How many noble and great men, loved and admired by their family, by their neighbors and by their loved ones, have ceased to worry about the difficulties of life and its trials when the one who subjugates kings, conquers tyrants, the destroyer of the unjust, tore them from their loved ones in cries, separating them from their family and their brothers without the latter being able to help them or protect them from the inevitable?

How many nations have been struck by death and how many cities have been brought to their knees? How many women have been widowed, children orphaned, and companions abandoned?

Thus, the wise man does not aspire to a fleeting situation as we have mentioned.

He does not forget that the inevitable will happen one day about which there is no doubt that it will happen.

Death is a swift hunter from which there is no escape and who cannot be slowed down.

Al-Kurayzi recited this poem to me:

Our goods are amassed for our heirs

We establish our roles in the destruction of time

Souls are overwhelmed by life here below and they are aware

That we must abstain from it to be safe there

Holding on doesn't save you from destruction

Just as flight does not protect you from annihilation.

Certainly ! Allah, the Noble and Most High, created Adam and his descendants from the earth.

Then he made them walk on it, eat its fruit and drink its rivers.

Then the fate of death inevitably approaches them.

This is when they become unable to walk and move.

Their bodies begin to fail.

Then, they return to the earth from which they were created.

It eats their flesh just as they ate its fruit.

It drinks their blood just as they drank from its rivers.

It dismembers them just as they walked on it.

The grave is the first stage of the afterlife and the last stage of life here below.

Blessed is he who has prepared himself for a comfortable grave throughout his life and has accumulated good works for his afterlife.

Ibrahim ibn Yazid said: "I saw a Bedouin standing by a grave and he was saying: Each person has a grave for their death.

Their number is decreasing and the graves are increasing.

You see a living house become deserted and a new grave appear for the deceased in the courtyard.

They are therefore the neighbors of the living: their resting place is near and their meeting is distant.

Conclusion

In this book I have mentioned some of the many texts that I hope will lead the reader to take on the behaviors and qualities of people of knowledge and wisdom.

Those who walk the path of the people of knowledge will find success and prosperity simply by meditating on their path and putting it into practice.

I did not include the chains of hadith transmission or the references to the quotes and poems, because I thought it was not necessary, just like the one who indicates a thing and urges that one does not is only interested in meaning.

May Allah place us among those who will receive the good news of success in fulfilling obligations with the aim of obtaining mercy from Allah and reaching the place of His close ones.

Indeed, this is the ultimate goal of believers and the greatest hope of those who are close to Him.

May the blessings of Allah be upon Muhammad, the Seal of the Prophets, and upon his pure and pious family.

All praise belongs to Allah, Lord of the worlds.